Guatemala: False Hope, False Freedom

'The President of Guatemala does not wear prison uniform, but he is a prisoner. The military, his gaolers, the country's gaolers, have given him permission to enter the National Palace. He has given them a promise of impunity for their killings and has assured them that he will not commit agrarian reform or any other sin.

The subject of this book is the mask worn by a circus democracy or, rather, the face which the mask hides — the reality of Guatemala, the reality of Latin America.'
Eduardo Galeano

Guatemala: False Hope, False Freedom

The Rich, the Poor and the Christian Democrats

James Painter

Catholic Institute for
International Relations

Latin America
Bureau

LONDON

5886
29.6.88

First published 1987
Catholic Institute for International Relations
22 Coleman Fields, London N1 7AF
and
Latin America Bureau (Research and Action) Limited
1 Amwell Street, London EC1R 1UL

British Library Cataloguing in Publication Data

Painter, James
    Guatemala: false hope, false freedom.
    The rich, the poor and the Christian Democrats.
    1. Guatemala — Politics and Government — 1945-
    I. Title II. Catholic Institute for International Relations
    972.81' 052   F1466.5
    ISBN Cased 0-946848-72-6 (CIIR)
    ISBN Paper 0-946848-71-8 (CIIR)
    ISBN Cased 0-906156-32-7 (LAB)
    ISBN Paper 0-906156-31-9 (LAB)

Cover and text design by Jan Brown Designs
Cover photo: Joe Fish
Printed in England by The Russell Press Ltd, Bertrand Russell
House, Gamble Street, Nottingham NG7 4ET

Distribution in the USA by Monthly Review Foundation

Contents

List of Boxes and Tables

 *Preface*

Many people forget that in Guatemala we are killed in two ways. One is direct repression, which has taken the lives of thousands of our brothers and sisters, and continues to do so. The other is hunger and poverty. These too are killing Guatemalans every day. Many people in our country have not had the opportunity to grow up, and those who have grown up have not had the opportunity to develop and live like human beings.

In Guatemala it's no good just looking at the personalities in political office because our problem is not a person or a political party, but the reality of a system of oppression, of exploitation and the plunder of resources. This system has enriched a minority in power, but also results in hunger and destitution for our people.

An army of repression was created to defend the wealth and interests of the minority. With all its force, hatred and intelligence, it opposes the rising of a people which refuses any longer to tolerate the consequences of this oppression. The Guatemalan army defends the whole system and so puts into practice a counter-insurgency strategy which aims, not merely to check the armed revolutionary movement, but also to crush any kind of development in the popular organisations. That is why the army has militarised our communities and villages, that is why it prevents rural workers from organising freely, and that is why it continues to use its repressive measures, including psychological warfare, against all our people. The army also directly attacks our cultural roots, our people's way of life and thought, and tries to implant the ideology which makes people accept the system of domination. We have to understand that the war against the people isn't just waged with bombs.

The installation of President Cerezo's government is an important part of the efforts of those who dominate us to ensure that the system continues. Vinicio Cerezo didn't win the election because he was very popular, but because the people were tired of the army. Both he and his party always knew what was to be their role in the army's power plan, which is a plan shared by other dominant groups in our country and in the rest of Central America. Vinicio Cerezo has kept a space for himself with the military because he has never been, and never will be, a threat to the system. That is why he is President.

The civilian government is giving the military more time, legitimacy, money, and a political space internationally which in the past it had no chance of obtaining because of its bad reputation and isolation. It's true that the people hoped that the civilian government might bring about genuine change which would give the people an opportunity to meet their basic needs. For example, they hoped for a minimal agrarian reform, a little piece of land or the chance to return to their native country where they had lived for centuries, without military control, in peace, without persecution. They hoped for an end to the disappearances, the kidnappings and the murders — for no more deaths. These are their deeply felt demands. They are the basic conditions for building our future. So far we have had no response.

The people have been making very practical demands because they have very practical needs. They want an end to the militarisation of the communities, and the re-establishment of the *cofradías*. These confraternities are an expression of the communal dimension of the people's religion, but the army regarded them as a form of popular organisation, considered them dangerous and attacked them as it did the popular organisations, with direct repression or infiltration.

Many people also believed or hoped that Vinicio Cerezo and the Christian Democrats would act as mediators in the people's struggle. But we have to understand that the struggle is based on the people's needs and the reality of the situation, not on abstractions. It is based on realities such as the pain of hunger, or seeing those responsible for the killings, the torture and the disappearances — far from being judged or punished — still acting against the people. The same system remains in place — a system which bears hatred against a people who want to live, the rule of a minority who will never share with the people what is rightfully theirs.

Nevertheless, the most important thing is that now is a time when the Guatemalan people are reaffirming their struggle, when they are reaffirming that they were not wrong when they created their own organisations and built them up. They are reaffirming the justice and necessity of a struggle which has already cost many lives, even though they know perfectly well that the army too is making its preparations. Our people are poised to make new advances because they have already set out on a journey full of pain, but also full of hope for a lasting solution to their plight. No-one will hold them back because they have come to realise that the solution is not in the hands of their oppressors but in their own hands. Their strength and their organisation will ensure that, though the journey may be long and difficult, peace will no longer be a dream but will become a reality.

Rigoberta Menchú
April 1987

Introduction

'Guatemala has become a normal country. It is a drastic change and most improbably, it looks like lasting. Five years ago, nobody would have predicted that Guatemala might achieve such a happy condition.'
The Economist, 14 June 1986.

'The clowns have changed, but the circus remains the same.'
Guatemalan priest quoted in *Le Monde Diplomatique*, June 1986.

Almost a decade has passed since the Latin America Bureau last published a book on Guatemala. The book's title, *Guatemala: Unnatural Disaster*, pointed to the irony of the fact that while the earthquake which left 22,000 dead in February 1976 attracted a flood of journalists and TV crews to Guatemala City, few paid any attention to the 15,000 who had died between 1970 and 1974 at the hands of right-wing terrorist groups. According to the book, 'many more had died from malnutrition resulting from the grossly inegalitarian land-tenure system and the unequal distribution of wealth and opportunity.' It is hard to believe that in the ten years that followed the publication of *Unnatural Disaster* both the political violence dealt out by military regimes and the crushing poverty that lies at the root of the violence became, if anything, worse. As the country plunged into full-scale civil war, the potential for development work by overseas agencies rapidly diminished. The programmes of many UK development agencies, including CIIR, were forced to contract or close down altogether.

Large numbers of peasants, trade unionists, religious workers, students and intellectuals turned to armed opposition groups — which later united to form the URNG (Guatemalan National Revolutionary Unity) — as their only escape from being trapped between the pincers of economic strangulation and political suffocation. By the beginning of the 1980s the URNG was capable of mounting a serious challenge to the state. The army's response was to launch a campaign of terror that has been rarely paralleled for its savagery (and lack of publicity) in the history of Latin America. The resulting carnage was so vast that at least another 30,000 Guatemalans have been killed, hundreds more have been 'disappeared', 440 Indian villages have been wiped off the map, and between 100,000 and 200,000 children have lost at least one parent. Over the same period, many of the social conditions that lie behind the dirge of statistics have deteriorated: real incomes have dropped, levels of malnutrition have probably increased, and the gap between the rich few and the poor (and largely Indian) majority has widened.

But there has been one important change. Thirty-two years of virtually unbroken military rule formally ended in January 1986, when the Christian Democrat leader, Vinicio Cerezo, was swept into office with a large electoral majority. The elections received a good dose of international attention and approval, especially for being free of fraud. This was seen as a welcome — and surprising — departure from recent electoral history in Guatemala, since in the previous three elections the military's rules for the game ensured that a presidential candidate could win the vote, but not the count. But the praise extended further. In a characteristically bold equation of elections and democracy, the US State Department triumphantly described the elections as 'the final step in the reestablishment of democracy'. The Reagan administration was quick to label the new government 'another example of democracy sweeping the region', in its attempts to further isolate the 'totalitarian' Sandinista government in Nicaragua. One could be forgiven for thinking that the elections by themselves were sufficient to introduce a new era of freedom and justice for the Guatemalan people.

Mr. Cerezo has also gained a considerable amount of international support and acclaim from a wide range of European and Latin American governments. Most have welcomed his victory for the advantages offered by a cleanly elected civilian President promoting a foreign policy of 'active neutrality' in Central America, which complements their own efforts to find a peaceful solution to the problems of the region. Thus, Cerezo's opposition to Reagan's pursuit of a military overthrow of the Sandinistas has found plenty of support from the Contadora Group and other Latin American countries, Western European governments, the Socialist International and even Fidel Castro. The renewal of full diplomatic relations between Great Britain and Guatemala in December 1986 — suspended since 1963 over Guatemala's claim to Belize — also has to be seen as a feather in Cerezo's cap. After a decade of ostracism of Guatemala by the international community because of its appalling human rights record, Cerezo is successfully using his foreign policy to usher the country back into the 'family of civilised nations'. But the elections and Cerezo's laudable foreign policy have acted as a mask for the lack of substantive change within Guatemala. As one Guatemalan commentator has expressed it, 'Cerezo sounds like a centre-left liberal abroad, while acting like a cautious conservative at home.'

In contrast to the universal optimism that has greeted Cerezo's victory, *Guatemala: False Hope, False Freedom* argues that the outlook for the majority of Guatemalans under the Christian Democrat government remains bleak. This is for two fundamental reasons. The first is rooted in the nature of wealth and poverty in Guatemala. In a highly polarised Central American society like Guatemala, can a 'centrist' Christian Democrat government — if it can even be called 'centrist' — provide real improvements for the poor majority when it is unable, or unwilling, to confront the interests of the rich and powerful? The second deals with the more immediate question of what could reasonably be expected of any civilian government coming to power after such a long period of military rule, and whether Cerezo has exceeded or lived up to those expectations. The answer to both questions leaves little doubt that the poor are not the winners — nor are they likely to be — in Guatemala's new 'democracy'.

Chapters 1 and 2 measure the chasm separating the rich and the poor, and, more importantly, explain some of the reasons for it. There are, of course, many other Latin American — and third world — countries where economic violence is an everyday fact of life, forcing thousands of families to live in grinding poverty; where governments put nearly all their resources into promoting export crops for first world consumers, while hundreds of children suffer, and sometimes die, from severe malnutrition; where the labour of vast numbers of ordinary people, no matter how great their energy and skill, is not allowed value above subsistence level. But the poverty that enslaves the majority of Guatemalan people has a claim to be considered unique.

Three main arguments justify such a claim. The first is the degree of inequality of resources and incomes. For example, a famous 1982 study by the US Agency for International Development (USAID) revealed that Guatemala has the most unequal ratio of land distribution in Latin America. Virtually all the country's high quality land and manufacturing assets are owned or controlled by a few hundred Guatemalan families, who for years have treated the country as a limited company. Guatemalan generals too have turned themselves into a caste of millionaires. Despite the secrecy with which the rich surround the details of their wealth, Chapter 2 introduces some of the families and generals who dominate the economy, and the systems which ensure their continued domination. Placed side by side with the poverty of the majority, the spectacular opulence of the rich seems all the more outrageous.

The second argument is that Guatemala has the unfortunate record of coming bottom of the list according to various social indicators. The 1987 UNICEF report, *The State of the World's Children*, showed that Guatemala has the worst illiteracy rate in Central America, the highest number of infants with a low birth weight, and the lowest percentage of pupils enrolled in the education system. Yet Guatemala is one of the richest countries in the region, possessing vast expanses of fertile land, oil and mineral deposits, and a relatively well-developed industrial base that until recently exported a significant part of its output. Explanations of why most Guatemalans remain so poor are not simple, but are a combination of interlocking factors some of which are outlined in Chapters 1 and 2: the emphasis on production for export at the cost of staple food production; increasing land concentration in the hands of the few and the corresponding lack of sufficient land for ever larger numbers of peasants and rural workers; the low wages paid to the permanent and seasonal workforce; and the handsome profits that those who control the land reap from the export of commercial crops.

The third reason why Guatemala is in a class of its own lies in the fact that it is a country divided not just by disparities in wealth, but by race. Between 50 and 70 per cent of the population are the pure-blooded descendants of the original Mayan inhabitants of Mesoamerica, while the remainder are *ladinos* (of mixed European and Indian descent). As in South Africa or Namibia, there is more to poverty than material deprivation. David Hamburg of the New York Carnegie Corporation wrote the following in the *Financial Times* of 19 April 1986:

> Poverty is partly a matter of income and partly a matter of human dignity. It is one thing to have a very low income but to be treated with respect by your compatriots; it is quite another to have a very low income and to be harshly depreciated by more powerful compatriots. To speak of impoverishment in this sense is to speak of human degradation so profound as to undermine any reasonable and decent standard of human life.

Hamburg was writing about South Africa, but he might have been speaking of Guatemala.

The ingrained discrimination against the Indian majority ranges from the concentration of wealth in *ladino* hands to the unashamedly racist attitudes of many *ladinos*. Although there are many poor *ladinos* and some Indians who have escaped the extremes of poverty by becoming traders, artisans or shopkeepers, it is *ladinos* who dominate the upper echelons of the economy. Indians also fare worse in their basic conditions of life: life expectancy for Indians is 16 years lower than for *ladinos* (45 years compared to 61); there is a higher degree of malnutrition among Indian children; and only 39 per cent of the Indian population is literate, compared to 61 per cent of *ladinos*. Racism is rife. *The Independent* reported on 3 March 1987, 'In a conversation with a European diplomat, a wealthy Guatemalan explained that the Indians were really just a part of nature. "Like plants and animals?" ventured the diplomat. "Exactly! Exactly," the wealthy Guatemalan replied.'

The racial divide is also relevant to any assessment of what elections might mean to most Indians. As one Indian woman catechist explained, 'The elections were for *ladinos*. They have radios, speak Spanish, and are therefore more in tune with what's going on. We indigenous people often do not speak Spanish, and are therefore less informed.' A story recounted by a journalist in the January 1986 issue of *Harpers* magazine, though sounding far-fetched, hints at the limits to electoral democracy: an Indian woman was observed voting during the 1984 Constituent Assembly elections. She was pondering the array of pictures on her ballot form, which was marked with symbols such as a bull's eye, a green tree and a dagger, so that those who could not read could recognise the different parties. 'She didn't know what to do,' wrote the journalist, 'but voting is mandatory; so she had to do something. Finally, in the margin of the ballot, she meticulously drew a spider, a bird, a cow, answering the pretty pictures with pictures of her own.'

Chapter 3 outlines the historical formation, ideology and social base of the Guatemalan Christian Democrat Party, and examines the party's response to the entrenched economic divide. It argues that the party has been through a slow process of dropping its reformist image and reassuring the traditional wielders of political clout in the country — principally, the private sector and the military — that it would not do anything to threaten their basic interests. This process reached its apogee before the 1985 elections, when the party's platform was defined by its, promise not to carry out measures that would clearly have benefited the poor and harmed the interests of the right — no agrarian reform, no serious tax reform, no nationalisation of the trading or banking sector, and no trials of army officers for human rights offences.

Despite the cautious programme of the Christian Democrat Party, there were high hopes after the elections that Cerezo would use his wave of support to carry out some reforms. Chapter 4 analyses the first 12 months of his government and argues that Cerezo has made it his priority to reach consensus with the army and CACIF, the main representative of the private sector. But the process of wooing the right has left him incapable of responding adequately to increased popular demands for land reform, jobs and wage increases. At the same time, as the army feels safe from prosecution, the climate of terror and the army's counter-insurgency campaign remain in force. The elections seem only to have acted as a smoke-screen for the continuation of the security forces' grisly operations and as a legitimation of the socio-economic status quo.

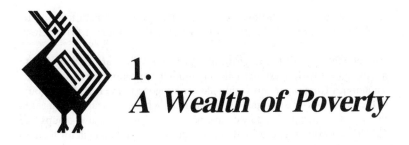

1.
A Wealth of Poverty

'I have faith and I believe that happiness belongs to everyone but that happiness has been stolen by a few.' Rigoberta Menchú.

At midday on 12 July 1986 a remarkable event took place in the small southern town of Nueva Concepción. At a rally attended by around 5,000 peasants, a portly, middle-aged Guatemalan priest, Father Andrés Girón, approached the microphone. In the full view of the nation's TV cameras, he shouted his solution to the peasants' poverty: nationwide agrarian reform.

Most observers could not easily recall the last time a public figure had dared to mention the unmentionable. Some even speculated that it may have been President Jacobo Arbenz, who over thirty years ago had implemented Guatemala's first (and only) major redistribution of land to around 100,000 peasants. Ever since Arbenz was overthrown in 1954 in a CIA-orchestrated coup, to call for a change in what is Latin America's most unequal pattern of land holding usually meant risking a visit from a death squad. Father Girón, too, was later to receive a series of death threats. But for the moment he was one of the few public voices denouncing the root cause of the country's poverty and social conflict — the problem of land use and land ownership.

Nueva Concepción lies in the southern department of Escuintla, right in the heart of Guatemala's fertile Pacific coastal strip. The region forms the backbone of the country's agro-export sector, where social disparities are at their most acute: eighty per cent of the region's land is concentrated in medium-sized and large farms devoted either to rearing cattle or growing export crops like cotton and sugar. Nearly half the population are landless wage labourers, providing a cheap workforce at harvest time on the huge plantations.

During his speech, Father Girón highlighted the particular problem around Nueva Concepción. He asked the visiting journalists at the rally to go and see for themselves the nearby plantations belonging to one of Latin America's largest landowners, Raúl García Granados:

'His plantations are today growing sugar cane. They are not producing anything for the *campesinos*. The only thing they produce for us is hunger. The money from sugar cultivation has always gone to the rich, is still going to the rich, and will continue to go to the rich. Why, in a sugar-growing area like Nueva Concepción, do we have no sugar? Why? Because groups like CACIF are exploiting the Guatemalan people. It is not enough for them to earn a few centavos — they want to suck us dry.'

The rhetoric was bold, but the facts bore him out. Raúl García Granados is one of Guatemala's wealthiest millionaires, whose fortune has been made in cotton and sugar cultivation. So extensive were his landholdings that in the 1970s he gained the reputation of being the third largest single landowner in Latin America. Although forced into exile in 1982 after a corruption scandal, he was widely believed still to have a controlling interest in 23 plantations in the area, covering around 7,500 hectares and mortgaged to a number of banks for US$108 million.

In contrast, many *campesinos** in the area could no longer afford to buy sugar. In the first six months of 1986 the price of sugar, like that of other main food items, had risen by around 50 per cent. Furthermore, thousands of workers who normally survived for a whole year on the money earned during the four months of the harvest were without jobs, as many cotton growers in the area had responded to the drop in world prices by changing to less labour-intensive crops, such as soya and sorghum. Those lucky enough to have a job found that fewer landowners were complying with the legal minimum wage of 3.20 quetzals (Q3.20 — about US$ 1.20 or 80 pence) a day because of the greater supply of cheap labour. Even before the inflationary spiral began in mid-1984, Q3.20 was widely considered to be insufficient to feed an average-sized Guatemalan family. Caught between the twin scourges of high unemployment and high prices, many Guatemalan families were existing at the margin of survival.

The area around Nueva Concepción is a microcosm of Guatemala's deeply divided society. While one man — who does not even live in the area — controls large tracts of land, vast numbers of poor *campesinos* struggle to eke out an existence. This chapter describes Guatemala's landscape of poverty, moves on to an explanation of the main reasons

---

* *'Campesino'* (peasant) is used loosely to include Guatemalans who farm a small piece of land and/or are hired agricultural workers.

for it, and then analyses how over the last five years most Guatemalans have become even poorer as a result of the economic disruption of the civil war and the country's worst recession for 50 years. The final section briefly examines what policies might begin to address the fundamental causes of such deep-rooted destitution.

The Quality of Life

According to a 1982 UNICEF study, no other Central American country is poorer than Guatemala. Combining the infant mortality, life expectancy and literacy rates into one criterion, it concluded that Guatemala had the lowest 'physical quality of life' index in Central America, and the third lowest in the whole of Latin America after Haiti and Bolivia.[1] All the relevant measures — income, health, malnutrition, educational standards and access to public services — suggest that only a very small percentage of the Guatemalan population does not suffer from the ravages of poverty.

The Guatemala-based independent weekly, *Inforpress*, has used government figures to estimate that in 1984 76 per cent of the population were poor — i.e. six million Guatemalans out of a population of eight million. Nearly 40 per cent, defined as 'extremely poor', could not afford a basic basket of food sufficient to provide an adequate protein and calorie intake, while another 36 per cent could afford the basket but not other essentials like proper clothes, shelter and transport. Separate calculations by the Government State Planning Council (SEGEPLAN) suggested that by the end of 1985 as many as 86 per cent of families were living below the official poverty line, and 55 per cent were 'extremely poor'.[2] The failure of the Christian Democrat government, elected in November 1985, either to halt price rises or to increase wages would suggest that even these figures would have increased by the end of 1986.

Rates of malnutrition are extraordinarily high, especially among young children under the age of five. A casual visit to the shanty towns of Guatemala City or the highland villages shows many children with the tell-tale signs of swollen bellies and skin diseases. Official statistics endorse the visual impression: the last national survey in 1980 found that only 27 per cent of all children between six months and five years old showed normal physical development according to the expected height by age, while 45 per cent showed a moderate or severe retardation.[3] Malnutrition has undoubtedly risen since the time of the study. Eduardo Meyer, the new Minister of Education in the Cerezo government, quoted a survey carried out by his Ministry which showed that in 1986 eight out of ten pupils who attended primary school arrived with an empty stomach.[4]

Whereas the top five per cent of income earners consume much more than necessary, the bottom half of the population are left with a grossly deficient diet. One 1978 study showed that the average person at the top consumed more than three times the calories, four times the protein, and six times the carbohydrates of the average person in the poorest half of the population.[5]

Guatemala has one of the poorest health records in Latin America. During a July 1986 visit, the head of UNICEF for Central America, Agop Kayayan, stated: 'Guatemala has the worst infant mortality rate in Central America. Every day 115 Guatemalan children under five — that's five children every hour — die from such diseases as diphtheria, whooping cough, tetanus, measles or polio.'[6] Infant mortality rates reached 80 per 1,000 in 1984 — comparative figures for the United Kingdom are around 12 per 1,000. Statistics for the rural areas and for the Indian population are much higher: one 1982 USAID study put the rate at 160 per 1,000 in the highlands,[7] while data for Indians are estimated to be nearly twice as high as those for non-Indians.[8] Given that most official figures predate the added devastation caused by the civil war, it did not come as a great surprise when Eduardo Meyer announced in early 1986 that the infant mortality figure in some areas was as high as one in five.

Perhaps the most outrageous statistic is that in 1981 — the last year for which government figures are available — more than 70 per cent of deaths of children between the ages of one and five were from easily preventable diseases: intestinal infections (the major cause of diarrhoea) represented more than a third (35 per cent), followed by influenza and pneumonia (18 per cent), measles (10 per cent), malnutrition (5 per cent) and whooping cough (4 per cent).[9] The sad reality is that the vast majority of child deaths could be prevented by adequate nutrition, vaccination programmes and proper sewerage and water systems. But Ministry of Public Health figures showed that in 1985 only two per cent of infants less than one year old (who are the most vulnerable to communicable diseases) had received a complete vaccination programme against the four main preventable illnesses.[10] However, it should be said that these figures do not take into account the possible effects of two UNICEF-sponsored 'vaccination days', carried out in May and July 1986 and estimated to have reached around one million Guatemalan children under the age of five.

Guatemala fits the pattern of most countries of the world in which low incomes and poor health go hand in hand. But it does not have to be this way. According to a 1985 Oxfam booklet on the record of the Sandinista government in Nicaragua:

During one of the first campaigns in 1981, over half a million under-fives were inoculated against polio and measles. In the following two years, not a single case of polio was reported, and measles dropped from being the fifth most common infectious disease to the thirteenth. Similarly, a three-pronged attack against malaria that year resulted in a 98 per cent fall in new malaria cases. [...] Whereas it is estimated that in 1979 little more than a quarter of the population could obtain medical services, by 1982 about 70 per cent of Nicaraguans had regular access to health care. In the process, there was a radical shift from primarily curative, urban-based care for a privileged minority to an emphasis on prevention.[11]

The fact that so many Guatemalan children die so young (in 1985 more than half the total number of deaths were of children under five[12]) is one of the main reasons why life expectancy is low. Another reason is the high percentage of Guatemalans who die from political or common violence — which accounted for an estimated 25 per cent of all adult male deaths in the early 1980s.[13] Although it has improved over the last two decades, life expectancy is still around 56 for urban Guatemalans and 41 in rural areas.[14]

One of the main reasons for such grim health figures is Guatemala's woefully inadequate medical and public health services (see box, pages 6-7). World Bank figures show that other countries with similar per capita incomes and fewer resources do a much better job.[15] The inaccessibility of many peasant communities, especially in the highlands, is an obvious obstacle to improving the percentage of the population with access to health care. Nonetheless, even when rural health centres are available, they are often poorly stocked, are closed because of the lack of medical personnel, or offer the wrong sort of treatment. One study of rural health practices carried out for the United Nations University in 1982-3 highlighted the various disincentives to attending the centre, including long delays, lack of respect for the traditional beliefs of the Indian community, and a tendency to hand out prescriptions for medicines, rather than the medicine itself. Many patients preferred to go straight to the local chemists, who offer both medicines and advice, or to traditional healers who prescribe low cost natural remedies and rites.[16]

The drugs that are available are often costly and inappropriate. Many *campesinos* simply cannot afford to pay for the prescription — in 1986 a common medicine against parasites cost about a day's wages, while a course of antibiotics could easily amount to a total week's wages. The general tendency to offer individual remedial services rather than community-wide preventive health care has often been criticised by international health organisations.

The Provision of Public Services in Guatemala

Health Care:

● 46 per cent of the population, equivalent to 3.67 million people, were without any access to some form of health care in 1985. In the same year the Ministry of Public Health and Social Assistance (MPSAS) covered only 22 per cent of the population.[1]

● There were 1.17 public sector hospital beds per 1,000 inhabitants in 1985 — occupation rates were between 51 and 66 per cent.[1] The figure for the United Kingdom is 6.43 per 1,000. In military hospitals, there were approximately 16.66 beds per 1,000 army personnel and their families.[2]

● 80 per cent of all health services are located in Guatemala City, although 61 per cent of the population live in rural areas.[3]

● Nationally, there is one doctor for every 5,000 inhabitants, and 70 per cent of doctors work in the capital.[4] Estimates vary for the rural areas from one doctor per 25,000 to one per 85,000 (in the highlands). The Guatemalan College of Doctors and Surgeons has estimated that there are more Guatemalan doctors working abroad, especially in the US, than in the rural areas of Guatemala itself.

Public Utilities:

● 54 per cent of houses had some sort of supply of drinking water in 1985. More than a quarter — and 39 per cent in communities of less than 2,000 people — took their water from rivers, lakes or springs. Only one in five homes in the smaller communities had running water.[1]

● In 1985 less than half (49 per cent) of homes had access to toilets, outhouses or latrines.[1]

● In 1980 there were only three plants of any significance for treating human waste, none of them in Guatemala City (which has 23 per cent of the total population).[1]

Housing:

● In 1985 there was an estimated housing shortage of 650,000 units, of ▶

The problem is also a lack of resources. Government spending on health over the last few years has represented only a small percentage of the national budget. Far larger amounts have been spent on defence and security and, in recent years, on debt repayments. Officially, military expenditure averages between 1½ times and twice as much as health spending, but unofficially it is much higher.[17] In order to stifle the URNG, military governments have spent more and more on defence at the expense of the health programme: from 1980 to 1983, defence spending rose by 26 per cent, while the health budget dropped which 325,000 were in the urban areas — roughly equal to the number of existing housing units. Each year 40,000 more units are needed for new families.[5] These figures are almost certainly underestimates, especially in the rural areas, where 'housing' for the majority consists of one-room makeshift shacks with dirt floors.

Social Security:
● In 1985 all the programmes of the Social Welfare Secretariat reached only 0.2 per cent of the population.
● In 1985 a little more than 25 per cent of the working population worked in centres affiliated to the National Social Security Institute (IGSS), which gives limited health care insurance and compensation in the case of working accidents or illness (but not dismissal) — it does not provide unemployment benefits.[1]

Education:
● Using the 1985 figure of 1,710,800 pupils of school age (i.e. 7-14 years old), Guatemala had one teacher for every 62 pupils, and one school per 215.[1]
● In 1986 there were an estimated 10,000 teachers without jobs and 800,000 school children without classrooms.[6]
● More than 73 per cent of those who began primary school in 1979 dropped out before 1984. In 1980-1, fully 42 per cent of the working population had no education at all.[7]

*Sources:*1. Government figures, usually from the Ministerio de Salud Pública y Asistencia Social (MSPAS), Dirección General de Servicios de Salud (DGSS), or SEGEPLAN.
2. *Central America Report* (London), Spring 1987, p.9.
3. Guatemala Health Rights Support Project, *Guatemala: Health Care and Hope*, Washington DC, p.2.
4. Guatemalan Human Rights Commission, *El Niño Guatemalteco en la Coyuntura Nacional*, Mexico City 1986, p. 11.
5. *Central America Report* (Guatemala City), 11 July 1986, p.205.
6. *This Week*, 21 October 1986.
7. Dirección General de Estadísticas, *Encuesta de Ingresos y Gastos*, 1980-1.

by 35 per cent.[18] The total amount available to spend on public services is also low compared to other countries, as a result of the refusal of Guatemala's wealthy to pay more taxes (see box, pages 32-3). Even when public investments are made, they tend to favour the urban areas and the agricultural export regions.[19]

Most Guatemalans do not fare much better when it comes to education. The 1981 National Census found that 46.5 per cent of the population over seventeen were illiterate. In the rural departments of Quiché and Alta Verapaz illiteracy rose to 78 per cent. The official figures are almost certainly underestimates, as they tend to include as literate those with only the most rudimentary writing skills — other sources put the illiteracy figure as high as 67 per cent of the total population.[20]

According to Eduardo Meyer, in 1986 approximately 2.3 million children, mainly in the rural area, received no formal education whatsoever owing to a shortage of schools.[21] Only 43 per cent of the population had completed the third grade. Absenteeism and early drop-outs are rife in the highlands, and the reasons are easy to identify: the lack of programmes for monolingual Indian children, inappropriate curricula and times for many children who have to work (and often migrate with their parents to find work), and the fact that many schools do not have classes beyond the third grade. One Indian *campesino* from a village in northern Chimaltenango aptly summarised the problem for many:

> 'When the kids reach fourth or fifth grade, many parents have to take their children away from the school because either they cannot afford the necessary text books and exercise books, or they need them to help them work. That's why most of the adults are illiterate because as kids they get taken away from school. The other main problem is that the language we speak mostly in this area is Cakchiquel. Sometimes the teachers only speak Spanish, so the poor child does not understand. Because they don't understand, the teachers think they are stupid and so the child gets really frightened.'[22]

Shocking as these statistics may sound, they should never serve to hide the social causes that lie behind them. The poverty of the majority of Guatemalans has not been compounded in the last ten years by any natural or ecological disasters such as prolonged drought or an earthquake; nor is Guatemala poor in natural resources, as it boasts some of Latin America's most fertile land and has abundant water resources. The main reason why most Guatemalans are so poor is a direct result of an unbridled 'free market' economic system that puts wealth into the hands of a powerful and privileged few and increases the poverty of the many. Ever since 1954 successive governments have not tried to change that system, which is one of the main reasons why the country exploded into civil war in the late 1970s.

The Roots of Poverty

'If we had the moral courage, we would not let a day pass without hearing the cries of the victims... the daily press would carry front page

pictures of children dying of malnutrition and disease in the countries where order reigns and crops and beef are exported to the American market, with an explanation of why this is so.' Noam Chomsky.

Land is the country's most important generator of wealth and poverty. Although in the 1960s and 1970s Guatemala began to develop a dynamic industrial sector, the mainstay of the economy is still agriculture. In 1984 it contributed 28 per cent of the Gross Domestic Product (GDP), and provided a livelihood for two-thirds of the population, including the vast majority of the poorest families. But Guatemalan agriculture is of two different types: on the one hand a few large commercial producers monopolise the best land, credit and other resources, while more and more peasant farmers are forced to survive on plots of land too small to support them — plots 'the size of a grave' in Eduardo Galeano's famous phrase.

Ever since the abandonment of the agrarian reform initiated under President Arbenz, economic growth has rested on the two per cent of farms which grow the bulk of the country's agricultural exports — especially coffee, sugar and cotton. The largest subsection is farms over 900 hectares — of which there are only 482 — occupying a colossal 22 per cent of Guatemala. On the other hand, 90 per cent of the country's farms — called *minifundia* — measure less than 7 hectares and are almost totally devoted to growing food crops like maize, beans, wheat and potatoes. The smallest of these (less than 1.4 hectares) represent 54 per cent of all farms, but only 4 per cent of all the farmland (see table, page 10).

The origins of this lopsided structure lie in the last century when coffee became the first of the modern cash crops. When Europeans developed a taste for coffee in the mid-1800s, *ladino* landowners and merchants were quick to take advantage of the new demand. The so-called Liberal Revolution of 1871 represented the rise to power of Guatemala's coffee elite, and the crop soon became the country's principal export earner. In the 50 years after the Revolution over one million hectares of national land were sold or distributed in individual plots to this coffee oligarchy, many of them to German immigrants who at the beginning of the century dominated coffee production from their base in Alta Verapaz. The main social effect of the Revolution was to establish large estates, which were the predecessors of the large coffee farms still to be found in many of Guatemala's 21 departments. The estates formed the basis of the coffee oligarch's economic and political power, and still do to this day.

These estates were not even a remnant of Guatemala's colonial past, as before the coffee boom there was a surprisingly low number of

Land Distribution, 1979

Farm Size (hectares)	Number of Farms	%	% (Acc*)	Area (hectares)	%	% (Acc*)
Less than 0.7	166,732	31	31	55,430	1	1
0.7-1.4	121,351	23	54	115,116	3	4
1.4-7	180,385	34	88	508,044	12	17
7-45	49,409	9	97	781,016	19	36
45-900	13,177	2	99	1,817,484	43	79
More than 900	482	—†	100	903,156	22	100
Total	**531,636**	**100**		**4,180,246**	**100**	

Source: Third National Agrarian Census, 1979.
*Acc = Accumulated.
†0.09%.
1 hectare = 2.47 acres.

large or even medium-sized properties. Nor were they the only, or most efficient, way of growing coffee. In Costa Rica, for example, there has been a long tradition of growers cultivating coffee at least as efficiently on smaller holdings. The main reason why these huge estates developed in Guatemala was because 'only large producers had enough political power to obtain forced labour, which was supplied by the state, and enough economic power to afford [the] production inefficiencies that use of forced labour entails.'[23]

The spurt in coffee cultivation also greatly increased the demand for seasonal Indian labour. To meet the demand, the government passed special legislation: the new laws were an attempt to force Indians to move to the estates by breaking up their communal land. They also resulted in forcing the Indians into debt to the coffee growers by advancing credit on condition that they worked for a fixed period of time on the estates. Forced labour was only finally abolished in 1944, largely because high rates of population growth had reduced labour shortages.

Nevertheless, the process by which Indians lost their land was accelerated by the rapid increase in new export crops after the Second World War. Cotton and sugar were introduced, and coffee production was increased. In general, large landowners boosted their agro-export production, not by improving yields per acre, but by increasing the amount of land they swallowed up. From 1950 to 1980, the amount of land devoted to cotton went up by 2,140 per cent, to sugar by 406 per cent and to coffee by 56 per cent. Beef production also increased by 2,125 per cent between 1960 and 1978. Large landowners increased

Children picking cotton in Tiquisate, Escuintla

Galera *on cotton farm, Tiquisate*

their holdings from 5.5 million to 6.7 million hectares, while the number of farms with less than 7 hectares jumped from 365,000 to 548,000, although the area they occupied remained more or less constant. The result was that the average size of small farms declined from 1.8 to 1.2 hectares.[24] The number of small plots (less than 0.7 hectares) rose the fastest — they more than doubled in number between 1950 and 1979, and came to represent 31 per cent of all farms.[25]

More and more *campesinos* were left without enough land to grow enough food to support themselves, especially in the western, mostly Indian, highland regions — the *altiplano* — which constitutes one of the worst pockets of poverty in Latin America. A 1980 USAID study of the *altiplano* concluded that 'nine out of ten people were living on plots of land too small to provide income sufficient to meet their basic needs'.[26] By 1980 the number of landless agricultural workers had risen to 420,000, while another 417,000 owned less than 3.5 hectares (3.5 hectares being the appropriate area of non-irrigated land to be worked by one family according to USAID). It was this rapid increase in the pressure on the land, and not 'Soviet-backed subversion', that, according to many analysts, was the main social factor behind the escalation of the civil wars in both Guatemala and El Salvador.

The small-farm households of the *altiplano* provide much of the temporary labour for the large agro-exporting estates in the fertile South Coast departments. Between 200,000 and 600,000 land-poor farmers or landless workers are forced to migrate every year in order to supplement their meagre incomes. Living and working conditions on the plantations are particularly appalling for women and children and have not changed for generations (see box, pages 14-15). This system of migratory labour is a key characteristic of the highly polarised Guatemalan social structure. Whereas in Honduras, Nicaragua and Costa Rica 'family farmers' (who own between 7 and 35 hectares) form around 20 per cent of the rural population, in Guatemala (and El Salvador) they constitute only around 6 per cent. Consequently there is a much greater gap between the few large estates and this vast mass of impoverished small producers and landless labourers.[27]

Recipes for Impoverishment:
Much of the poverty and malnutrition flows from this archaic land tenure system, and the emphasis given to export-led development which maintains and enforces the inequalities. Four issues are often pinpointed as the main ingredients in Guatemala's recipe for poverty: 1) unequal development; 2) low wages in the agro-export sector; 3) food crops neglected in favour of export crops; and 4) the absence of agrarian reform.

1) Unequal Development

In the 1960s and 1970s the Guatemalan economy boomed, with an average annual growth rate of 6.8 per cent, which was more than double the population growth rate of 3 per cent. However, as the upper echelons of the economy are controlled by a narrow group of landowners, industrialists, financiers, and traders (see Chapter 2), there were enormous obstacles to the benefits of the economic growth 'trickling down' to the poor.

In fact, there is little evidence to suggest that any trickling down occurred, except perhaps to Guatemala's small middle class. USAID studies in 1970 and 1980 both concluded that the situation of the *campesinos* worsened in absolute terms over the previous decade.[28] That is to say, it was not just a case of the gap between the rich and the poor increasing, but of each year the poor surviving on less income, land and food. At the same time, income distribution, already highly concentrated, became more so. In 1970 the wealthiest 20 per cent received 47 per cent of the national income, 55 per cent in 1980 and 57 per cent in 1984. The poorest 50 per cent had 24 per cent in 1970, 20 per cent in 1980 and 18 per cent in 1984.[29] Disparities in the rural areas were extraordinarily acute: Ministry of Economy figures for the early 1980s show that 83 per cent of the rural population received around 35 per cent of the total rural income, whereas the two per cent who owned more than 35 hectares of land received five per cent more — i.e. 40 per cent.[30]

One of the main reasons why income remains so concentrated is the very low level of taxes paid by the Guatemalan rich. Even when the economy was booming in the 1960s and 1970s, tax revenue did not keep up with the rate of growth.[31] As will be seen in Chapter 2, the levels of taxation — described by the *Financial Times* as 'ludicrously low'[32] — permit high levels of profits and little revenue for the state. As one development economist expressed it, 'poverty in Guatemala is not a product of the absolute poverty of the country but of the present structure of income: it could be substantially alleviated with appropriate polices of redistribution.'[33] But the political obstacles to such redistribution are enormous. As one US Embassy official in Guatemala neatly summed up the problem: 'My very good friends in CACIF are with the government in power. Therefore it is understood that they will not pay taxes to whatever government is in power.'[34]

2) Low Wages in the Agro-export Sector

Wages on the plantations which generate the country's wealth remain very low. There are three basic reasons why this happens: the over-supply of labour, the absence of an internal market, and the absence of

Slave Labour

One of the most popular postcards on sale to tourists in Guatemala City depicts three fair-skinned Guatemalan women picking coffee, dressed in brilliant and spotless indigenous costumes. The colour of their lipstick neatly matches the bright red of the coffee berries. The back of the card reads '*indígenas cortando café*' which is translated as 'natives gathering coffee'. It would be hard to imagine a more distorted image of the reality of coffee-picking. Most of the women pickers on the coffee estates are Indians, many of whom are are forced by their poverty to travel with their husbands and children to the plantations at harvest time. Rigoberta Menchú was one of them:

'Mothers are very tired and just can't do [the picking]. This is where you see the situation of women in Guatemala very clearly. Most of the women who work picking cotton and coffee, or sometimes cane, have nine or ten children with them. Of these, three or four will be more or less healthy, and can survive, but most of them have bellies swollen from malnutrition and the mother knows that four or five of her children could die. We'd been on the *finca* for fifteen days when one of my brothers died from malnutrition. My mother had to miss some days' work to bury him. Two of my brothers died in the *finca*. The first, he was the eldest, was called Felipe. I never knew him. He died when my mother started working. They'd sprayed the coffee with pesticide by plane while we were working, as they usually did, and my brother couldn't stand the fumes and died of poisoning.'[1]

Women represent around 25 per cent of all the temporary wage labour on the coffee plantations.[2] On top of the picking, they often have to do the cooking in the *galeras* [open sleeping barns] in which they are housed with the rest of the temporary workers. These *galeras* usually have dirt floors, no beds, no side walls and no nearby access to running water or sanitary facilities. Some of the highest malnutrition levels and child death rates are to be found on the plantations. One recent study of 602 Indian women who were resident workers on ten plantations found that over a certain period there had been 2,424 live births but a staggering 645 deaths — for 127 seasonal women workers the figures were 656 live births and 170 deaths.[3]

The reckless use of pesticides (particularly on cotton plantations) is a particular problem for mothers. A famous 1978 INCAP study showed that Guatemala had the highest reported levels of DDT contamination of mothers' milk in the entire world: out of a sample of 81 women living in different parts of Guatemala, only one had lower than the recommended limit. On the cotton plantations the levels were between 12 and 244 times the acceptable minimum.[4] Why the heavy use of insecticides? In the words of one of the landowners: 'It's very simple: ▶

more insecticide means more cotton, fewer insects mean bigger profits.'[5]

In 1976 a paper was presented to the UN which claimed that the transport and working conditions were so appalling and the labour recruitment methods of such dubious legality that the whole system of migratory labour could be justifiably compared to that of slavery.[6] A *contratista* [contractor] usually lends money in advance to peasant farmers who use it to buy corn or fertiliser. In return the peasants have to work on a *finca* for a fixed period, and the loan is automatically deducted from the wage.

A personal visit by a foreign journalist to a coffee and cardamom *finca* near Nuevo Progreso in San Marcos in September 1986 revealed that little has changed in the ten years since the UN paper. She picked coffee on the *finca* with a group of 50 migrant workers from villages near Sacapulas, Quiché who were on a one-month contract:

'The families live all together in a *galera* which consists of roughly planked walls, a dirt floor, and no furniture except some hammocks and posts to hang bundles on. They are being paid Q4.20 (about £1) for every 100 pounds of coffee they pick, but they are only able to pick 30 pounds a day. Some of them, even after working a whole month, are not going to earn enough to pay off the *contratista* who had lent them the money to buy the fertilizer they need for their *milpas*, so they are still going to end up in debt. The adult workers receive only two pounds of corn and four ounces of beans per day, which they must share with their children. The rest of their food they have to buy from the closest town (several kilometres away) or from the permanent workers on the farm.

The woman who does the cooking for the workers migrates to the farms every year with her husband and three children. They have ten *cuerdas* [about one acre] of land in Quiché, but in their own words 'they have to have paid work to have something to eat in the summer.' She goes to bed at 7 p.m., gets up at 1 a.m. to prepare the breakfast for the rest of the workers, and then takes them out their food at lunchtime. For that she and her husband (who cuts the wood) earn Q6 between them (75p each) a day.

The owner of the *finca* is said to be a military man or a *judicial* [member of the secret police] — he also owns two other *fincas*, a new white helicopter, a new Cherokee, and a large chalet on the beach near El Salvador.'[7]

*Notes:*1. Extracts from Rigoberta Menchú, *I...Rigoberta*, Verso, London, 1984, chs. VI and VII. 2. Rokael Cardona, 'Caracterización del Trabajo Temporero', *Perspectiva* No.1, Guatemala, August 1983. 3. *Cultural Survival Quarterly*, Spring 1983, p.18. 4. Marit de Campos (INCAP), in ICAITI, *Seminario Regional sobre el Uso de Plaguicidas*, Guatemala City, 1978. 5. *Estudios Centroamericanos*, San Salvador, June-July 1978, p.465. 6. Roger Plant, *Guatemala: Unnatural Disaster*, Latin America Bureau, London, 1978, p.82. 7. Author's correspondence.

easy alternatives for many *campesinos*.

The supply of an unskilled and low cost permanent and seasonal labour force tending to outstrip demand has depressed wages. Although reports by the International Labour Office (ILO) and USAID have often pointed to the low wage rates as one of the major causes of poverty,[35] the legal minimum wages set by governments are inadequate and often evaded. Wage increases have been very rare and even when they occur, they are not sufficient to keep pace with the rise in the cost of living. After a strike by 70,000 sugar and cotton workers in 1980 (which cost the lives of many of its leaders), the minimum salary was raised from US$1.19 to US$3.20, but only after landowners had been assured in private that it would not be enforced.[36] Even though as a result of this wage hike the average rural wage rose in nominal terms from US$0.95 in 1972 to US$2.35 in 1982, after taking into account inflation, the US$2.35 was only worth US$0.86 at 1972 values.[37] Even during times of high world prices for Guatemala's export crops such as in the 1970s, the higher revenue was not shared with the workers. Between 1973 and 1979, real wages on the cotton, coffee, sugar and banana estates dropped 20 per cent.[38]

The thousands of Indians and poor *ladinos* who pick the coffee and the cotton serve the economy only as a source of cheap labour, and not as consumers. It is foreigners, mostly in the rich industrialised countries, who consume the products. As a 1983 report by the Washington Office on Latin America (WOLA) explained it:

> In economies which have developed an internal market, it makes business sense for employers to strike a balance. The people who work in their factories or in their fields are also their consumers. If they are paid too little, they will buy less, and the employers' income will fall. Prosperity depends on walking a line between controlling production costs and putting enough money into consumers' pockets to maintain a healthy demand for goods and services. Under the Guatemalan structure there is no incentive to put money in the hands of workers and, as a consequence, wages are forced down to starvation levels.[39]

According to some analysts, Guatemalan export agriculture has also developed differently from that of the neighbouring countries of Nicaragua, Costa Rica and Honduras. As there was more undeveloped land available on the so-called 'agricultural frontiers' in the latter three countries, it was more difficult for commercial producers to monopolise resources. As a result they were forced to attract labour by offering wages high enough to compete with the income peasants could earn as small producers.[40] Because of the greater demographic

Rates of Growth in Population and Agricultural Production, 1950-1980

Years	Food Crops %	Agro-exports %	Total Population %
1950-1960	2.1	9.7	4.1
1960-1970	3.8	5.1	3.6
1970-1980	3.0	7.8	2.8
1950-1980	**3.0**	**7.5**	**3.5**

Source: Food and Agricultural Organisation (FAO) Year Books.
Note: Food crops include rice, beans, maize and wheat. Agro-exports include cotton, coffee and sugar (although between 30 and 50 per cent of sugar goes to the home market).

pressure on the land in Guatemala and a greater supply of labour, agribusiness could more easily develop using the poor *minifundistas* and the excess supply of labour without having to pay higher wages.

3) Food Crops versus Export Crops

Over the last thirty years Guatemala has produced more and more crops for first world consumers, but production of the food that most Guatemalans eat has tended to stagnate. The basic diet of the majority of Guatemalans consists of maize, rice, beans and wheat, which in the early 1980s provided more than two-thirds of the available calories and 60 per cent of the available proteins. More nutritional food like milk products, eggs, fruit or vegetables do not figure in most people's diets, partly because there are few rural families who have enough income to afford them. But while the agro-export sector grew at an average rate of 7.5 per cent between 1950 and 1980, the growth in the staple four crops only averaged 3.0 per cent, which was not enough to keep up with population growth (see table above). Even though per capita corn and bean production did slowly improve in the 1960s and 1970s, from 1965 to 1975 there was an increase of 50 per cent in the number of children under five suffering from malnutrition.[41] This was because better consumption depends not only on improved per capita production but on how many people have enough income and/or land to eat sufficient quantities of food.

Guatemala fell into the trap of producing more and more of what it did not consume, and consuming more and more of what it did not produce. The failure to give greater incentives to food crop production led to greater reliance on food imports, which became an increasing drain on scarce foreign exchange. In 1965 Guatemala imported 11 per cent of its cereal requirements (93,000 tonnes), but this had risen to 17 per cent by 1980 (247,000 tonnes). Moreover, in the ten years between 1970 and 1980, the cost of all Guatemala's food system imports jumped from US$56.5 million to US$313 million — equivalent to 21 per cent of the value of all Guatemala's exports for that year.[42]

The main obstacle to improved food production was that, as previously mentioned, the four basic food crops were grown by *minifundistas*, who live on the worst land, benefit from little technical assistance, and either suffer usurious credit terms or receive no credit at all. In fact the modernised agro-export sector hogged the major share of the scarce commercial credit dispensed by the banks. Between 1956 and 1980 it received 80 per cent of all the agricultural credit, while much of the remaining share going to food crops went to the large farms growing these crops.[43] For example, in 1981 cotton-growers received US$500 for every hectare cultivated compared with US$20 per hectare for the production of maize. As for beans, they are grown almost exclusively on small farms by producers who received credit worth only one per cent of the value of their produce, in contrast to 50 per cent in the case of cotton. Large farmers can offer a greater security to the banks that the money will be repaid, while small farmers can offer little or no collateral against a loan. In their desperate search for credit, smallholders are often forced to make payments in kind to the larger producers, who end up acting as intermediaries for the banks.[44]

4) No Agrarian Reform
The landed elite has forcibly and bloodily opposed any expropriation of the source of their wealth. So, since 1954 the main mechanism for alleviating landlessness has been a pitifully inadequate land colonis-ation scheme (see box, pages 100-1). Most of the handouts under the scheme took place on untitled land owned by the state, usually situated in the frontier zones in the Petén and northern Alta Verapaz, the so-called Northern Transversal Strip (FTN). These parcels were often inappropriately large, apparently in order to establish commercial, middle-sized farms under USAID guidance, and often went to politicians or the military. According to a 1980 World Bank report, the opening up of new lands in the FTN had actually resulted in a 'substantial distribution of large blocks of land to persons from the middle and upper income classes'.[45]

Contrary to popular belief, Guatemala does have an Agrarian Reform Law. Decree no. 1551, passed in 1962, allows in certain circumstances for the expropriation of unused land in farms over 100 hectares. But a labyrinth of bureaucratic obstacles has meant that no appreciable amount of cultivable land has ever been expropriated since the law was passed. According to USAID estimates, in the whole of the country there are 3 million acres of idle land, the vast majority of which is found on the large estates.[46] A tax on idle land is meant to encourage the large landowners to bring this unused land into production, but this has been easily circumvented. USAID estimated that in 1979 alone the tax that should have been paid on idle land amounted to US$900,000, but in the whole of the period from 1970 to 1981, the National Institute for Agrarian Transformation (INTA) collected only US$600,000. In 1981 the sum INTA received was a paltry US$22,000. INTA has been much more attentive to collecting payments due on the parcels of land that had been distributed under the colonisation scheme. Over the same period from 1971 to 1980 INTA received US$5.3 million from the beneficiaries — i.e. nine times the figure paid in taxes on idle land.[47]

It should be stressed that these four 'recipes for poverty' have been selected for an introductory understanding of why most Guatemalans remained caught in the poverty trap. A more complete analysis would at the very least mention the failure of the industrial sector to absorb the excess supply of labour from the agricultural sector, its domination by a number of families and individuals who can monopolise the channels to credit and foreign capital, and the high rates of return enjoyed by local businessmen and transnational companies (TNCs). But the major problem has been the shortcomings of the export-led model of development. These were not so much the instability of the prices paid for Guatemala's main exports, although this did not help. Nor is there anything intrinsically wrong with a country growing crops for export in order to earn the revenue to pay for its imports. But in Guatemala there were two fundamental reasons why the poor got poorer under the system: first, the benefits of the growth in agro-exports went disproportionately to a narrow band of the rich; and second, the rapid development of the export sector occurred at the expense of the smallholder economy growing the food most Guatemalans eat every day.

At root, the dominant system was almost totally 'free market'. Decisions about what to grow were made on the basis of private gain, and enough food was only granted to those who had sufficient income or land to afford it. But probably the simplest, but biggest, obstacle to alleviating poverty remained political. In the 1960s, 1970s and early 1980s hundreds of poor workers and peasants who began to organise into unions, cooperatives, or political-military groups in an attempt to escape from their poverty were killed. Some of these killings were carried out by landlords employing para-military bands. The bloodshed had a certain logic to it that stemmed from the predominant model of development. If land was expropriated and given out to peasants, not only would the oligarchy probably lose some of their land but they would also run the risk of being forced to raise wages (and therefore lose profits) in order to compete with peasant farm income and maintain a regular source of cheap labour.

The Poor Get Poorer 1980 – 1985

'Whereas before they were killing us through physical violence, what we're suffering now is economic violence.' Indian woman coffee-worker from Retalhuleu, July 1986.

In 1980, Guatemala plunged into its worst economic crisis for half a century. This coincided with the most savage years of the army's counter-insurgency programme in the highlands. The net result of both was to compound the poverty of many of the poorest.

When the industrialised countries went into recession at the end of the 1970s, the repercussions on the Guatemalan economy were immediate. There was a sharp cut in the price of and demand for the country's main agro-exports. There was also a major contraction of Guatemalan sales of industrial goods through the Central American Common Market (CACM). Frightened by the political instability both inside Guatemala and in the rest of Central America, the private sector was too scared to invest and instead shipped large amounts of capital abroad. The military government of Lucas García tried to compensate for the lack of investment by stepping up work on large-scale 'white elephant' public works projects. This compounded the foreign debt (partly because of the rampant corruption of the military) and rapidly increased the fiscal deficit, already swollen by the cost of fighting the war.[48]

At the start of the 1980s economic growth slowed and then went into reverse. From 1980 to 1985 half of the economic growth of the previous 30 years was lost, and GDP per capita slumped to the level of 1971.[49] The value of agro-exports fell from US$880 million in 1980 to US$580 million in 1985, while that of food crops dropped from Q555 million to Q475 million over the same period. The social effect was devastating: 38 million work days were lost in the rural economy and Q113 million less was paid out in wages.[50] Outright unemployment increased fivefold from 1980 to 1984, so that by 1985 at least 45 per cent of the working population did not have a full-time or permanent job. As the cushion of unemployment benefit does not exist in Guatemala, most of the unemployed simply turned to the already swollen informal sector. Regular visitors to Guatemala City could observe the rapid increase in the number of justifiably insistent vendors and beggars who stalked the restaurants and streets.

For those who still had jobs, wages remained fixed at 1980 levels. These were: Q3.20 (US$1.20 or 80 pence) per day in the agricultural sector, Q3.95 (US$1.50 or £1) in industry and Q3.48 (US$1.30 or 90p) in the commercial sector. Even in 1982 — before inflation took off — average real wages of Q3.51 in the urban areas and Q2.35 in the rural areas covered only about half the cost of the daily minimum diet.[51] Although the Guatemalan economy has historically enjoyed very low rates of inflation, this all changed from about mid-1984 onwards. Artificial shortages, the rapid devaluation of the quetzal and the growth of the parallel and black markets were mainly responsible for a rise in the Consumer Price Index of 35 per cent between August 1984 and September 1985.

What affected the poorest families hardest was the rise in the price of basic food items. In 1985 alone the price of maize and beans increased three-fold. Guatemala's small professional middle class also suffered from the job losses and declining real salaries. The least affected were the rich, partly because they spend an insignificant portion of their income on food and could much more easily absorb the food price rises.

Nowhere was the effect of the recession more keenly felt than on the south coast. By 1985-6 the number of migrant workers from the highlands had dropped to an estimated 200,000. This was partly because of the restrictions on movement as a result of obligatory service in the civilian patrols, partly because of the knowledge that fewer jobs were available, and partly because many Indians preferred to stay in the highlands for security reasons — to migrate was often equated with 'fleeing' and therefore suspect in the minds of the army. Nevertheless, there was still a large reserve supply of labour in most areas: an estimated 100,000 had fled to the south coast in the early 1980s and settled there semi-permanently for fear of being killed if they returned to their villages. In the period 1982-3 jobs were so scarce in some areas that many Indians turned up at plantations begging to be allowed to work merely in exchange for food to allow them to survive.

Andrés Coj [name changed] was one Indian who fled with his family from his village near Santa Cruz del Quiché after army repression in 1982. He ended up on a large *finca* called 'Madre Mia', 15 kilometres to the north of Retalhuleu, and did not dare to return to his village:

'We stayed on the *finca* and lived in a *galera* for three years. Can you imagine — 60 of us living all year round in a *galera* without any walls? Every time it rained, the water came pouring in. The only thing we had was a roof above our heads — no medicine, no doctors, no school. We even had to walk 15 kilometres if we wanted to go to mass. There were around 600 of us who worked on the *finca* all year, and about 1,000 more at harvest time. We were paid around Q3.20 a day during the cotton harvest, but that wasn't enough — especially after the rise in the cost of beans and maize. I reckon during my time on the *finca* around 20 children died of hunger or malnutrition.'[52]

Andrés was not typical. At least he had a job. Many displaced and migrant workers could not find work even at harvest time. Many landowners responded to the drop in world demand and prices for their export crops by switching to new crops like soya or sorghum which need less manual labour. The effect of the recession was most dramatic in the case of cotton. Cotton absorbs a lot of labour in the harvest months of November, December and January. In the early 1980s cotton production crashed because of low world prices and the rising costs of the necessary imported inputs. By 1986 the situation was critical. According to Alfredo Gil Spillari, head of the National Cotton Council, only 20,000 hectares were sown with cotton in 1986, compared to 120,000 at the end of the 1970s and 70,000 in 1985. As he himself explained, 'Two years ago cotton growers paid out Q72 million in wages to day workers, which benefited 56,000 families. This year because the price of a quintal of cotton has dropped by more than half, 42,000 hectares are being given over to growing sorghum, maize, sugar cane and for rearing cattle.'[53]

The effect on job opportunities was disastrous. Cotton needs 83 workers per *manzana* [= 0.7 hectares], while the other crops need only two or three per *manzana*, so the move to less labour-intensive and more mechanized crops meant that 28,000 day workers were left without jobs in 1986.[54] One priest from the big cotton-growing area of Tiquisate claimed that the whole area had been given over to soya and sorghum production:

'Everything is sown, grown and picked by machine. As a result this year we're going to have between 25,000 and 30,000 workers without jobs in this zone alone. And what are they going to do with the soya and sorghum? They're going to make oil and chicken-feed. But what are they going to do with all the temporary workers who depend on working on the cotton plantations for four months a year? They're not going to eat.'[55]

It was depressingly common to hear from plantation workers that during 1986, because of the recession, many employers were taking on fewer workers or increasing the amount of work that had to be done for the same wage (see box, pages 24-5). Many workers, especially on smaller farms, continued to be paid less than the legal minimum. If Q3.20 was considered an insufficient income to feed a family properly in 1980, it is not difficult to imagine what it bought in 1986 after the rapid rise in the cost of basic food items. There was little incentive for employers to pay more as the excess supply of labour continued to hold wages down. 'I get all the men I want for Q1.50 a day,' explained one *ladino* coffee planter in August 1985, 'I have to turn them away.'[56]

Some south coast *finqueros* were also using brutal methods against *colonos*, or permanent resident workers, who still lived in semi-feudal conditions on their estates. Although from 1964 to 1979 the percentage of *fincas* on the south coast with *colonos* had dropped from 38 per cent to 4 per cent, there were still as many as 50,000 living in the four southern departments of Escuintla, Suchitepéquez, Retalhuleu and San Marcos.[57] The landlords' justification for expelling *colonos* was to reduce costs: it was far cheaper to employ labour on a temporary basis than to have the cost and obligations all the year round of 'supporting' a *colono* family. One method of expulsion was simply to tear down the strips of corrugated iron from the roofs of *colono* houses. If this was not sufficient, some landowners were said to have burnt down the houses in which many families had been living for generations. One church source claimed that Roberto Alejos — notorious for allowing mercenaries for the Cuban Bay of Pigs invasion to train on his soil (see page 44) — was one such landlord. Some also claimed that day workers were not being offered the customary free handouts of beans and tortillas, which they now had to buy or cook for themselves. This of course was a double blow, as not only did they now have to spend more of their wages but the price of maize and beans had also risen so sharply.

The Cost of War

On 5 January 1986 the Guatemalan daily *Prensa Libre* published a photograph of an emaciated Indian boy, propped up in a hospital bed. The boy's skin hung from his skeleton-like figure. Underneath the photograph a simple caption read: 'This is not Biafra nor Ethiopia. This is not Africa. This is happening in the highlands of Guatemala.' The accompanying text was that of a speech given by a Guatemalan journalist to mark the end of 'Youth Year 1985':

During the electoral campaign when candidates paraded themselves in the media, they were always accompanied by young university students, who

---

The Luxury of a Cough
Interview with Indian catechist from Retalhuleu, July 1986

Q: What are workers whom you know being paid this year?
A: I would say that the average daily wage is around Q2 [50 pence], but some pay only Q1.50. For example, to clean two to three *cuerdas* of land [about one-third of an acre], you'll get paid Q2, but the difference is that they're now paying by the *tarea* [i.e. by the job] and not by the day. When you pick the coffee, you get from Q2 to Q2.50 per *molde* [a type of large container]. In previous years you had to ensure the *molde* was full, but now it's got to be overflowing! Whole families work all day from 7 a.m. to 4 p.m., and then at the end of the day the administrators will still cheat you over the weight you've picked or chuck out two or three pounds saying they're dirty.

Q: So, in general, conditions are worse this year?
A: Yes, I would say so. There's much more hunger around. In many *fincas* the *voluntarios*[1] are not given any food, so they have to go and buy it from the nearby village. With the rise in the prices, and because they are not paid very well, they simply cannot afford to buy enough to feed themselves. If you have ten in your family, you need five pounds of maize a day[2] which at 25 cents a pound now costs around Q1.50 — that's before the beans and everything else you need. Very often families only eat in the morning and evening, and miss lunch. The contracted workers will get something at lunchtime, but it's usually only a few tortillas. Because there's more hunger this year, there's more malnutrition and so more people are susceptible to diseases.   ▸

---

were handsome, well-dressed and overweight. None of them concentrated on the real dimension of the problems affecting young people in Guatemala right now. We need to think of what has been done for the thousands of teenagers who are living traumatised by the violence in the highland mountains of Quiché, Huehuetenango and the Verapaces. There, I insist, young people are dying of hunger, from malnutrition, without any clothes, without schools, without health care, and, to top it all, as orphans because the violence has destroyed their homes.

Despite the scarcity of information detailing the full effects of the army's counter-insurgency campaign on the highland economy, and despite the army's claim to have brought 'development' to the area, the worst cases of malnutrition were still to be found in the highland villages. Numerous human rights reports have detailed the unbridled savagery of the Guatemalan army's counter-insurgency campaign from 1980 to 1983 but few noted the economic crisis facing the

Q: What sort of diseases?
A: Malaria especially. There's very few medicines available. Even if you can get a prescription it costs Q8, so what are the people supposed to do with it — chew it? We say that to have only a cough is a luxury.

Q: Is there any change in the conditions on the *fincas*?
A: No, people are still living in the *galeras*, sleeping on the floor. We often say that the sheds for the cattle are better than the *galeras*.

Q: What happens if you protest?
A: The *finqueros* have lists of people who protest or who are known trouble-makers. If you're on the list, you're told you can't work on the *finca*, so you don't protest. Many people who come down from Huehuetenango and Quiché are on the list because they're suspected of 'being involved in politics'. They have to pass from *finca* to *finca*, trying to find work. In many cases they don't return to their villages — or if they do, only with an illness and no money. Sometimes they just end up abandoned. They die simply out of starvation, or because the weight of their sorrow breaks their hearts.

[1] *Voluntarios* are semi-permanent workers, to be distinguished from *colonos* (permanent resident workers), and *cuadrillas* (migrant labourers).
[2] The State Planning Council recommends a minimum of just under a pound of maize per person per day, supplemented by a variety of other foods, to ensure a healthy diet.

survivors of the holocaust. The initial effect of the army's terror tactics and scorched earth strategy was to leave vast areas of maize-growing land either burnt down or abandoned. One 1983 survey of the rural areas of Chimaltenango revealed that 16 out of 27 villages studied had no harvest in 1982, because they had simply been abandoned — only five had enjoyed a normal harvest.[58] The miserable situation facing the *campesinos* was compounded by the demands of civilian patrol duty which often did not allow for travel to the south coast nor adequate time to work their *milpas* [cornfields]. This made grain supplies scarce and expensive, and more Indians became dependent on army food handouts. Food became a very important political weapon for the army, both to control the Indian population and to starve Indian survivors out of the mountains.[59]

The food supply did improve in 1985 and 1986 although a 1985 WOLA study by two US anthropologists reported that 'general shortages [did] remain and in some areas, including the 'model villages' and other places where people remain separated from their lands, shortages [were] more acute.'[60] The prospect for the thousands of Indian families attempting to rebuild their shattered lives and homes remained very bleak. In many cases peasants were not allowed to return to their former plots of land, while traditional sources of income had dwindled. Few could sell handicrafts because of the decline in tourism, while both the opportunites for waged labour on the south coast and the wages paid had been cut drastically.

One peasant farmer from a small village in northern Chimaltenango explained that in 1986 there was still a significant shortage of maize in his area. Land still lay abandoned after previous army sweeps, and because of the lack of sufficient income to match the rise in the price of fertilisers. As a result, 'instead of cultivating and trying to improve the land, the people now have to go and work in other areas to earn the money to buy the maize from outside the village.'[61] There were also reports of some families in the highlands having to survive on one meal a day, or being forced to supplement their diet with boiled weeds. A 1986 Americas Watch report wrote that 'so poor is the diet in highland peasant households that the directors of a child feeding program in northern Quiché, which provides hot meals for some 200 children, found that when the program closed for three weeks in December 1985, children returned in January in the first and second stages of malnutrition.'[62]

For those living in the army-controlled model villages, the food supply was in general more secure, mainly as a result of the large donations of food given to the Guatemalan army by international agencies like the UN's World Food Programme and USAID's PL480 programme. But the long-term prospect was not good. The model villages, and the 'development poles' of which they formed part, were, in essence, a form of social control. They were not economically viable. As the same WOLA study concluded, 'The [army's] program is virtually all security and not development. There is development potential in a few naturally rich areas, but no real prospects for development in most of the model villages. In the Ixil triangle, the program actually undermines the development potential and may be creating new problems.'

Perhaps the one ray of hope was the fact that some Indian families who had remained in the mountains after fleeing from the army had managed to grow new crops under extraordinarily hazardous conditions and keep themselves from starving. By growing *malanga* (a type of tuber) instead of maize as it is less detectable by army air sweeps, and slowly introducing primary health care and literacy classes, some Indian survivors were shaping a type of 'development' that at least was under their own, and not the army's, control (see Appendix).

Policies of Hope

Reading of such wholesale hunger and poverty often provokes only despair or, at best, sympathy for the poor. But policies do exist which would begin to address the underlying reasons why most Guatemalans remain so poor. Just before the 1985 presidential elections *Inforpress* published a detailed study, identifying three key measures that would help relieve poverty in Guatemala:[63]

1) A broad agrarian reform

This could reduce underemployment, improve income distribution, make peasant farmers less reliant on seasonal wage labour, and help to create a stronger internal market to stimulate domestic manufacturing. With an agrarian reform, Guatemala could also probably reduce the amount of money it has to pay for imported food. It could also stem the increase in the numbers of landless, and thereby improve political stability.

2) Nationalisation of foreign trade and banking

This would curb the foreign exchange shortage resulting from exporters hoarding their dollars in foreign banks, help government control over the flow of dollars and allow government to direct investment to more socially useful ends.

3) An overhaul of the tax system

This would change the relative importance of direct and indirect taxes, increasing the proportion of direct taxes so that the higher income groups would contribute the bulk of tax revenue. At present, the 'consumer' taxes fall disproportionately on the poorer sectors. More of the wealth of the rich would be used to cover expenditure on the expansion of economic and social services for the poor.

Political reality in Guatemala is that parties, leaders or movements advocating such policies are liable to be labelled 'communist subversives' and risk disappearance or death. For the last three general elections no party has included an agrarian reform, a wealth tax or nationalisation measures as part of its electoral platform.

Nowhere was the absence of these measures more noticeable than in the 1985 presidential elections. Despite the depth of the economic crisis, despite the devastation caused by the war, and despite the lessons of the previous thirty years of 'development', none of the major parties, not even the Christian Democrats, advocated any of the three policies in their electoral campaigns. They were hardly discussed by any of the major contenders, and if they were mentioned, it was only to reject them as 'irresponsible'. In many other Latin American capitalist countries such policies have been the platform of moderate and mainstream parties. However, Guatemala's new 'democratic process' still meant that social reforms were off the political agenda. The nearest equivalent in British politics would be an effective veto on the participation of the Labour and Alliance parties in an election on the grounds that they proposed serious tax increases on the wealthy.

Other non-governmental organisations have recommended additional policies that could be adopted by any government committed to alleviating poverty:

● A 'food first' policy that could ensure that all Guatemalans have enough to eat, including a reorientation of credit, technical assistance and public spending, and a system of price subsidies.[64]
● A legally-enforced increase in minimum salaries and an encouragement of labour unions. This would distribute more equitably the cost of any stabilisation plan or the benefits of any growth.[65]
● For those highland families devastated by the war, a massive injection of humanitarian aid for food, shelter, clothing and medicine. Also, 'pre-development' aid for seed, fertiliser, thread and tools should be supplied via private or local level public sector organisations with autonomy from military control.[66]
● Rigorous price controls and a ban on luxury imports for the rich.[67]

However, in the first twelve months of the new Christian Democrat government none of the policies listed above was adopted or pursued in a serious fashion, as Chapter 4 will argue. Agrarian reform — which for many is the litmus test of the seriousness of any government's commitment to the poor — was categorically ruled out by the new president. Instead, his government would rely on new flows of foreign aid and renewed economic growth, largely based on the reactivation of the agro-export sector. But economic growth, especially when it depends on improved agro-export production, is not in itself a solution. Without an attack on existing patterns of income and land distribution, the benefits of any growth will continue to be monopolised by a minority. The 1985 elections seemed doomed only to confirm the lesson of recent Guatemalan history: the main function of the vote was to keep intact a frozen and unjust economic status quo.

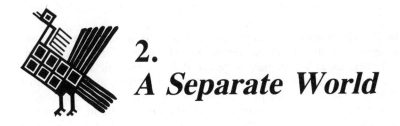

2.
A Separate World

'CACIF's view of the world remains simple and uncompromising. "I got through my work and efforts what I wanted; no-one can touch it and others can starve at my door."' Professor Piero Gleijeses, John Hopkins School of Advanced International Studies.

A 15-minute bus ride from the centre of Guatemala City is all it takes to visit the separate world of Guatemala's wealthy elite. In Zones 14 and 15 private guards lounge aimlessly outside luxurious mansions that boast well-watered lawns and roofs topped with US$5,000 satellite dishes to catch US television. Backing on to part of Zone 14 lies a sprawling shanty town, which is conveniently shielded from the view of the residents by a 20-foot wall. There poor Indian and *ladino* families cling to existence in bamboo and corrugated iron hovels without running water or sanitation. The cost of the satellite dish alone would be the equivalent of the joint annual income of at least 15 of these families. The wall stands as a stark symbol of the sharp divide in Guatemalan society, which even the US Embassy recognises as suffering from 'striking inequalities' in income distribution and land ownership.[1]

The previous chapter argued that for any government to implement policies like a tax or agrarian reform that would alleviate the desperate poverty of the majority, it was necessary to confront the entrenched interests of the wealthy few. This chapter therefore describes who the rich are, what they are defending and how the economic system works in their favour. Put simply, there are three colossi who have dominated the Guatemalan economy and society since the overthrow of Arbenz in 1954.[2] Together they form the basis of economic power in the country:

● **A Guatemalan *ladino* elite,** whose wealth was based historically on coffee, but which since 1950 has moved into industry and new agro-exports like cotton, sugar, cattle and, most recently, non-traditional products.

● **The Guatemalan security forces,** who were originally trained and equipped by the US in the 1960s, but who now, like Frankenstein's monster, exhibit a degree of political and economic independence from their creators. The army are in general fiercely anti-communist, they favour free enterprise, and are the ultimate guarantors of oligarchic interests. In contrast to their counterparts in El Salvador and Honduras, since the 1960s a series of top military officers have used their control of the state to expand the army's own economic base into agro-export, industrial, finance and real estate interests.

● **A variety of US transnationals and banks,** many of whom directed Guatemala's industrialisation process in the 1960s and 1970s, often using national elites as junior partners. These companies have links with the traditional ruling families, the military, and the economic and political agencies of the US government.

The three colossi are not altogether separate groups as their economic interests overlap. There are also times when important divisions have surfaced both within and between them. These tensions became more noticeable at the end of the 1970s, when the economic crisis and civil war momentarily threatened their very survival. The joint Chamber of Agriculture, Commerce, Industry and Finance (CACIF), which, rather than a political party, acts as the main voice of the private sector, has been racked by internal splits both between 'traditional' and 'modernising' agrarian interests and, more recently, between coffee, cotton and sugar growers and commercial and industrial groups. For example, in the Ríos Montt period CACIF nearly split apart after the introduction of tax measures that clearly favoured the agro-export sector. There have also been frequent battles between CACIF and the military: whereas CACIF has always advocated decreased government spending, an end to military corruption and the privatisation of various public companies (in which the military have a large stake) as a solution to the country's fiscal problems, the military argue for increased taxes on the private sector. Nonetheless such conflicts, though clearly important, have always tended to be secondary to a united and unwavering defence of the economic status quo and a rejection of social reforms.

The Fruit of the Land

Despite 30 years of industrialisation and diversification of the

Agro-Export Production by Farm Size, 1979

Agro-export	Value ($m in 1980)	Total No. of farms	% produced on farms > 92 has. (no. of farms)	% produced on farms > 1840 has. (no. of farms)
Coffee	464	97,679	83% (3,651)	19% (188)
Cotton	166	331	100% (309)	38% (49)
Sugar	69	16,854	95% (1,250)	41% (91)
Cardamom	56	12,267	68% (645)	13% (82)
Bananas	45	23,133	83% (1,900)	3% (31)
Beef	29	117,595	70% (8,166)	22% (337)

Source: Third National Agrarian Census, 1979.
Note (1): Most large landowners own more than one farm, so production is even more concentrated than in the table.
Note (2): Between 30 and 50 per cent of sugar is consumed domestically.

Guatemalan economy, land remains the major source of wealth. The traditional agrarian oligarchy has slowly been replaced by, or adapted into, a more modernising and capitalist agrarian elite, which represents the most important and powerful sector of the Guatemalan bourgeoisie. The elite's huge agro-export enterprises generate three-quarters of the country's foreign exchange and employ up to half the salaried work force. The production of each major cash crop is controlled by a limited number of families or producers (see table above), who receive the lion's share of the foreign exchange earnings. These families enjoy the best land and the easiest access to credit and capital. They pay very few taxes to the state (see box, pages 32-3) and reap the benefits of high profit returns.

With easy access to loans and with the political unrest in the region, a large proportion of these profits are not invested productively but spent on luxury goods or shipped abroad to fatten Miami bank accounts. Even before the escalation of the civil war, a 1980 World Bank report concluded that 'a substantial portion of [the foreign exchange earnings] leave the country to pay for the importation of consumption goods and for investment or other expenditures abroad. A significant share is also held domestically in relatively non-productive forms such as land held for speculation.'[3] In the early 1980s capital flight was so extensive that in just five years Guatemala lost more than US$1.1 billion in foreign exchange just to the US — equivalent to nearly half Guatemala's total foreign debt in 1984.[4]

The lifestyle of this agrarian elite is, by any standards, comfortable. Usually domiciled in Guatemala City, they often leave the running of

---

Taxing Questions

'The tax bill has become a question of fundamental principle for many people here. If it cannot be passed or if it is emasculated, then it will mean that nothing really basic can be done in Guatemala — that those who have wealth will not yield something to those who have nothing.' *New York Times* reporter, 1966.

The Guatemalan rich pay less tax than virtually any other elite in the Western hemisphere. Their unwillingness to support government expenditure has left Guatemala with the lowest tax ratio in Latin America except Haiti: tax income as a percentage of GDP amounted to 5.3 per cent in 1984, while the average for Central America ranged from 12 to 31 per cent. Successive military regimes have turned to the poor to raise more income. From 1970 to 1986 direct taxes on income and property (which affect upper income groups, while indirect taxes fall most heavily on consumers) comprised on average less than one-fifth of all tax revenue (see table), whereas for most countries with market economies the figure is closer to 80 per cent. Income tax provides an average of 40 per cent of government income in Europe, 22 per cent in Brazil, but only 13 per cent in Guatemala. Over 80 per cent of the direct tax in Guatemala comes from income tax (both personal and company). Property taxes are low (they represented only 0.9 per cent of total government revenue in 1980), as landowners have proved themselves so adept at understating the value of their land. Property tax evasion also makes land a very attractive investment for the wealthy at times of high inflation since land tends to hold its value.

Exporters too pay few taxes and are notorious for tax evasion. Between 1970 and 1976, taxes on coffee exports amounted to 10.0 per cent of the value of declared export earnings, on bananas 4.0 per cent, on cotton 1.3 per cent, on sugar 4.4 per cent, and on beef virtually nothing. After 1977, taxes paid on all exports did rise and peaked at US$158 million in 1978, but the amount began to drop rapidly in 1981 with the recession and crashed to US$29 million in 1984 and only US$10 million in 1985. As one Inter-American Development Bank (IDB) official recently summarised the whole taxation system, 'generally speaking, the rates are low, exemptions are generous, and evasion is substantial.'

Government attempts to increase taxes have been fiercely opposed ►

---

their *fincas* to administrators and the security of the premises to private armed guards or pay-rolled members of the Mobile Military Police (PMA). As unionisation and strikes on the *fincas* are both rare and dangerous, the workers have no means of securing a large enough share of the cash crop income to rise above the threshold of survival. The 'planter mentality' that fiercely defends such inequalities consists

Government Revenue 1970-1986
(in millions of quetzals)

	1970	(%)	1975	(%)	1980	(%)	1985	(%)	1986	(%)
1) Direct Taxes										
a) On Income	18.7	(13)	54.7	(18)	92.1	(13)	108.0	(16)	134.1	(10)
Personal	4.3		12.7		23.6		35.8		39.4	
Company	14.4		42.0		69.5		72.2		94.7	
b) On Property	6.0	(4)	8.9	(3)	7.1	(1)	17.6	(3)	27.8	(2)
c) Other	—	(—)	0.1	(—)	3.0	(1)	0.6	(1)	3.0	(1)
Total Direct Taxes	24.7	(17)	63.7	(21)	102.2	(15)	126.2	(19)	164.9	(13)
2) Indirect Taxes†	117.7	(83)	237.2	(79)	594.7	(85)	553.1	(81)	1139.3	(87)
Total Taxes	142.4	(100)	300.8	(100)	696.7	(100)	679.3	(100)	1304.2	(100)
Total Gov. Revenue	163.2		329.8		747.3		864.8		1509.4	

Source: Guatemalan Central Bank
†Indirect taxes include taxes on foreign trade, petrol, alcohol and tobacco, and stamp duties.

by the private sector, and especially by landowners. One of the reasons for the August 1983 coup against Ríos Montt was private sector annoyance at his 10 per cent value added tax on non-essential consumer goods, which Mejía Víctores reduced to seven per cent soon after taking over. In April 1985 the Mejía government announced a package of measures including a 15 per cent tax on non-essential imports from Central America and a 50 per cent tax on goods from outside the region, but CACIF immediately demanded the withdrawal of the measures and the resignation of several Cabinet ministers. At first Mejía stood firm, but after rumours of a coup, he rapidly cancelled a planned visit to the Middle East, rescinded the taxes and dismissed the Finance Minister.

In their defence, businessmen either claim that they would pay more taxes if no state corruption could be guaranteed or argue that an increase in taxes would act as a disincentive to invest and therefore lead to more unemployment. But the reality is, as one foreign diplomat recently put it, 'the private sector does not seem to want any kind of responsibility for the development of the infrastructure or for the well-being of the population as a whole.'

of a mixture of unashamed racism towards Indian workers; a 'never again' attitude towards the agrarian reform and militant trade unionism of the Arbenz period; and a rabid defence of the free market system, claiming that it benefits all Guatemalans.

A 1984 Minority Rights Group report on Guatemala's Indians quoted one rich landowner, who replied to his daughter's concern at

Guatemala City

Guatemala City

an outbreak of coughing among Indian children on his plantation with the observation: 'They're not children, they're Indians.'⁵ Other landowners display a keener understanding of the advantages of a free labour market. A 1983 WOLA publication cited a 'representative planter' from a recent study of 122 plantation owners as saying, 'Unemployment is good for Guatemala. That is why you can earn two or three hundred dollars a month in Guatemala and still have enough money for a maid or two. If people are hungry enough they will work at anything.'⁶

Coffee: Bitter Harvest

More than 100 years after the Liberal Revolution coffee still forms the spinal column of the Guatemalan economy and the country's number one export. In 1985 coffee exports were worth US$450 million, equivalent to 42 per cent of total exports. Coffee is also the cash crop providing the most income to the government, and the major generator of employment in the country. According to a 1986 estimate by the coffee-growers' association, ANACAFE, more than half a million peasants and agricultural workers receive an income as a result of coffee production, and two million more benefit indirectly through their relation with other branches of the coffee process.⁷ But what ANACAFE did not say was that although there are thousands of small-scale coffee-growers and temporary coffee-pickers, it is only a limited number of coffee families who dominate the three stages of the Guatemalan coffee industry, namely the cultivation of berries, processing the berries and exporting the coffee beans through the export houses.

In 1979 there were 97,679 farms producing coffee in Guatemala, but only four per cent of these controlled 83 per cent of national production (see table, page 31). According to the US Department of Agriculture, these large estates are 'among the largest in the world.'⁸ One recent estimate was that one per cent of the growers produced 70 per cent of the harvest.⁹

But who are this one per cent? The major families tend to guard the secrets of their wealth, partly through fear of kidnapping attempts and partly through fear of having to pay more taxes if the full details of their landholdings were made public. Nevertheless, some of the best known coffee 'names' are Mombiela, Campollo, Flores, Aragón Quiñónez, Pivaral and Plocharsky in the departments of San Marcos, Quezaltenango and Guatemala; the Brol family in Quiché, the Peyre family in Escuintla and the Falla family around Antigua; and German names like Daetz Villela, Diesseldorf, and Thomae still with coffee interests in Alta Verapaz.

Some of these families, like the Mombielas, have not modernised nor diversified much from coffee, but the majority have both introduced new technology and turned to additional cash crops, which increasingly in recent years have been non-traditionals like cardamom, cut flowers, or processed agricultural goods. For example, the Falla family now export cut flowers, the Brol family grow cardamom in the Ixcán, while 40 per cent of the production of one of the biggest and most moderning coffee families, the Plocharskys, is said to be made up of non-traditionals. Some of the families have important links with the major banks that fund coffee production: José Falla was President of the Banco Agrícola Mercantil — Guatemala's fifth largest bank and a major source of credit for coffee-growers, as was Manuel Soto Marroquín, another major coffee producer in the department of Retalhuleu.

The large producers receive the bulk of the private bank lending, which allows them to use outside loans rather than invest their own capital to cover a high proportion of their annual production costs.[10] A minority of the 40,000-odd smaller producers receive some funding through the Guatemalan Federation of Coffee Cooperatives (FEDECOCAGUA), but all too often they are forced to turn to intermediaries linked either to larger producers or to one of the 32 privately-owned *casas exportadoras* [export houses]. Most of these export houses belong to the powerful Coffee Exporters Association, ADEC, in which some coffee-producing families like the Stahls have an additional interest through their ownership of an export company.

In general, the export houses exercise a remarkable degree of control over the whole coffee industry: as the only contacts for the brokers and import-jobbers in the consumer countries they enjoy a monopoly of the lucrative external marketing of coffee (in contrast to El Salvador there is no state marketing agency); they lend out more money than the banking system and finance as much as 70 per cent of national production by loans secured from abroad; and they control much of the coffee grown by the small producers in different parts of the country. This they do by dispensing loans at short-term, high-interest rates, the terms of which allow for expropriation of the borrower's land in the case of non-payment, and by using intermediaries or cooperatives to make the small producers sell their coffee to them at a low price, often fixed at the time of the loan.[11]

For some coffee traders and producers, large contraband sales to Mexico and Honduras and the practice of under-invoicing (to avoid taxes) have helped to swell already good returns and deprived Guatemala of a sizeable proportion of its principal source of foreign exchange. It is hard to estimate the scale of the loss to the state, but when two coffee scandals came to light in 1986 — one of which involved a personal friend of President Cerezo and former Minister of Agriculture, Iván Nájera Farfán — together they added up to Q12 million worth of illegal coffee sales.[12] But even 'legal' profits are generally considered to be high, helped in the last two years by favourable exchange rates. Under the military regime of Mejía Víctores, who was himself rumoured to be engaged in profitable coffee-dealing, coffee traders were allowed to retain 25 per cent of their earnings in dollars no matter what the international price. At the time the quetzal's parallel rate against the dollar was three times the official one. According to the *Financial Times*, this meant 'large black market profits' as coffee dealers reaped the benefit of the parallel rate.[13] According to one coffee trade magazine, the new Christian Democrat government's decision to devalue the quetzal in March 1986 and pay exporters at the rate of Q.2.50:US$1 gave the coffee industry an 'added windfall' for 1986 and 1987.[14]

More than any other branch of the Guatemalan private sector, the coffee oligarchs are by repute the most resistant to change. Historically the self-avowed 'party of organised violence', the MLN (National Liberation Movement), has articulated most vociferously the coffee-growers' recalcitrance, even to the point of condemning the Christian Democrat Party as 'Marxist' for its occasional advocacy of mild reforms. Héctor Aragón Quinonez, the erstwhile vice-president of the party and himself a major coffee-producer, recently dismissed the peace negotiations in El Salvador between President Duarte and the left-wing coalition FDR/FMLN as 'discussions between two sets of leftist guerrillas'.[15]

Although in recent years important differences have developed between the more modernising and liberal coffee-growers in the west of the country and diehard MLN supporters in the east, ANACAFE remains united in its resolute opposition to an expropriatory land reform. When Father Girón publicly demanded his nationwide agrarian reform in July 1986, ANACAFE was one of the many private sector bodies to immediately take out large paid advertisements and bombard the press and TV with declarations about the 'irresponsibility' of such a measure. 'No-one can question the right to private property,' claimed Rodrigo Rodríguez, the vice-president of ANACAFE in a 15 July press interview, 'even to think of expropriating land is an act of robbery.'[16]

The Cotton Club

Mayan Indians were already cultivating and processing cotton for their own needs at the time of the Spanish Conquest, but it was not until the mid-1950s that *ladino* producers started to grow cotton for export. In the 1960s and 1970s a new breed of cotton growers rapidly acquired land in the fertile areas of Tiquisate and La Gomera in Escuintla, where they were soon building small strips for their aeroplanes or helicopters to land during short stopovers on their huge plantations. While most of them remained residents of Guatemala City, the majority of Indian workers whom they employed did not even know their names.

The growing demand for cotton fibre on the world market, the building of new roads, and the discovery of DDT and other insecticides all contributed to boosting Guatemala's cotton exports. Total production rocketed from 15,000 quintals in 1950 to 2,160,000 quintals in 1978, while the area sown with cotton rose from 1,750 hectares to 120,000 hectares over the same period. By the end of the 1970s cotton had firmly replaced bananas as the country's second major foreign exchange earner, and Guatemala had become the fourth largest cotton producer in Latin America. But the main beneficiaries of the wealth generated by the cotton boom were a mixture of older families diversifying into cotton and a new group of entrepreneurial cotton growers, who were more risk-orientated than the traditional coffee-growers. Others who benefited were the landlords who rented them the land, the bankers who gave them a ready flow of credit to buy up or rent vast chunks of highly productive land, the merchants who sold the cotton on the world markets and the transnationals who supplied the inputs.

Of these, the tiny number of cotton-growing families undoubtedly benefited the most.[17] According to a 1985 study by the Economic Commission for Latin America (ECLA), when compared to other cotton-producing countries, Guatemalan cotton production displays two key characteristics: 'extreme concentration of landholdings and an absolute free market system of production.'[18] The 1979 census showed that 309 large *fincas* controlled 99.95 per cent of cotton production (see table, page 31), but this figure did not reveal the smaller number of families who owned the *fincas*. A 1980 study by the National University of San Carlos (USAC) reported that in 1977 a mere 47 families controlled 75 per cent of production, while just 15 families controlled nearly half.[19] In contrast to the coffee sector, there were virtually no medium-sized producers, so there was no need for intermediaries. In fact many of the families had an additional interest in the processing of cotton (often owning their own gins, textile mills or vegetable oil factories), while 14 mostly foreign 'traders' controlled the external marketing and enjoyed average profits of 4 to 6 per cent of the value of the cotton exported.[20]

In first place came the Molina family — most notably the two brothers Milton and Hugo — who were estimated to own 11,500 hectares around Tiquisate, equivalent to 10 per cent of the total amount of land sown with cotton that year. They also owned a cotton gin in the area. In second place came the notorious García Granados family, who owned 7,000 hectares and a cotton factory around La Gomera. Milton Molina was even said at one time to be the largest individual cotton producer in the world. Certainly, even in neighbouring El Salvador and pre-revolutionary Nicaragua there were a larger number of producers (around 1,600 and 2,700 respectively) for roughly the same area of cotton.[21] In 1979 the average size of a Guatemalan cotton *finca* was 638 hectares, whereas for Central America it was 25 to 40 hectares and for the rest of Latin America even less.[22]

Some of the older coffee-growing families also diversified into the various branches of the cotton business: the Alejos family were major growers, and owned two gins and a vegetable oil factory; the Herreras were also growers, and had investments in cotton textile mills and the Banco del Agro, which lent out credit to cotton growers; and the Aycinena family invested in cotton-growing and two cotton gins. Other powerful and enormously wealthy families like the Kongs, the Ibargüens and Zimeri were also involved in different phases of the cotton economy.[23]

The Ponciano family neither belonged to the traditional landowning class, nor owned as much land as the Molinas or Garcías, but it was a classic example of this new elite of cotton-growers, amassing a fortune in a very short time.[24] From 1965 onwards three brothers, Edgar, Roberto and Miguel Angel — two of whom were engineers and probably had no previous experience of agriculture — began to buy up land in Tiquisate that previously belonged to the United Fruit Company. They snapped up their first plantation of 472 hectares with an initial down payment of US$23,000, and the profits from the first harvest — estimated to be a staggering US$100,000 — helped them to buy their second *finca* the following year. Usually by buying out smaller producers, in seven years the three brothers acquired six plantations measuring around 1,500 hectares and at 1972 prices worth US$400,000 (or US$3 million at 1986 prices). The family also enjoyed their fair share of political influence: the father, Colonel Ponciano, was a presidential candidate in 1966 for the MLN, while Edgar Ponciano was a close friend of Raúl García Granados, who was then secretary of the Revolutionary Party (PR) and later infamous for his inside knowledge of the operations of the death squads. One of the

Ponciano brothers was also rumoured to be chief of the local death squad in Tiquisate.

Equally significant was the way the Ponciano brothers enjoyed easy access to credit from banks: they mortgaged their plantations one by one to secure more loans. From 1965 to 1975 they received around US$360,000 from the main Guatemalan bank financing cotton production at the time, the Banco del Agro. Thereafter they switched to the Banco Inmobilario — in which they were said to be major shareholders — and by 1977 their total borrowing had risen to more than US$550,000. In general the cotton kings were closely tied to the financial sector, in which the local banks were often owned by the same agro-industrial elite. Between 1966 and 1982, cotton, sugar and coffee received 65 per cent of all the credit available to agriculture (whereas basic food crop production received only ten per cent).[25]

The ease with which cotton-growers could borrow money meant higher profits: 90 per cent of the total cost of producing cotton was paid for by external financing, while only 10 per cent was covered by reinvesting profits. Twenty per cent of the costs came from foreign credits, usually from US banks, so that the cotton elite could afford the high percentage of necessary TNC-supplied inputs like fertilisers, pesticides and machinery. Pesticides alone absorb around 40 per cent of total costs, but only 5 per cent are produced in Guatemala.[26] The reliance on imported inputs also meant that the net contribution of cotton to Guatemala's balance of payments was noticeably low: for every dollar of exported cotton, 55.6 cents went out of the country to buy the inputs.[27]

Cheap labour, high productivity and low taxes also helped to guarantee good returns: in 1979/80 cotton wages represented only 10.3 per cent of total costs compared with around one-third for Argentina, Mexico, Paraguay and El Salvador; yields were the highest in Latin America and second only to Israel's in the world; and taxes on cotton exports seldom represented more than one per cent of the total value. One study, based on figures from the Bank of Guatemala for the cotton harvest of 1975/6, estimated pre-tax profits at US$62 million, nearly four times the US$16 million paid out in salaries.[28] Employers could easily have doubled the amount paid out in wages and still received a good return. Even in bad years profits still held up. In 1983/4 only 56,000 hectares were dedicated to cotton, largely because the price had dropped to around US$68 a quintal on the world market. Nevertheless, the results of the harvest were still 'positive' according to the Bank of Guatemala, by which it meant average pre-tax profits of US$410 per hectare.[29] This would have meant a US$23 million profit for the cotton club — still more than the US$17 million paid out to

30,000 cotton workers that year.

In 1986 the cotton growers' main lobby organisation, the National Cotton Council, responded to the cotton crisis by demanding emergency subsidies from the new Christian Democrat government. But since cotton, unlike coffee, has the fortunate characteristic of being easily replaced by other crops, many of the cotton-growers were able to absorb the worst effects of the crisis by changing to soya, sorghum or other non-traditionals promoted under the US-sponsored Caribbean Basin Initiative, which was designed to give preferential treatment to certain exports from the region to the US market.[30] As mentioned in the previous chapter, the real sufferers were the 28,000 cotton workers who were left without jobs as the new crops were much less labour-intensive.

The Sugar Kings

Sugar cane was the second major new cash crop to help fuel the growth of the Guatemalan economy in the 1960s and 1970s. Guatemala was a net importer of sugar in the early 1950s, but production soared after the Cuban revolution in 1959 when the US government decided to switch Cuba's sugar quota to Central America. US sugar imports from the region tripled in the 1960s and Guatemala was one of the main beneficiaries, as it was often allocated the largest Central American quota. To be more precise, it was not so much the country that benefited as the *finqueros* with the most capital, who were best able to use the better quality varieties of sugar cane to boost profits and yields, and the family-owners of the twenty *ingenios* [refineries], who controlled the most profitable branch of the sugar industry. The amount of land given over to sugar cane jumped five-fold between 1961 and 1976 from 15,000 to 76,000 hectares, while yields increased 63 per cent over the same period. By the mid-1970s well over half of the country's sugar was being exported and sugar had become the third major foreign exchange earner.

Like cotton, most of the sugar cane was grown on a limited number of large-scale plantations, mostly situated in the highly fertile and swelteringly hot Pacific departments of Escuintla, Suchitepéquez and Retalhuleu. In 1979 just 91 *fincas* controlled 41 per cent of production, while 1,250 (equivalent to 7 per cent of the total number of *fincas*) controlled 95 per cent. The refineries are conveniently situated in the heart of the sugar-growing areas and close to local paper, confectionery and spirits industries. All twenty of the sugar mills were privately owned, most commonly by some of the oldest and most powerful families in Guatemala, who unsurprisingly had other landed,

Top Ten Sugar Mills in Guatemala, 1983			
Name of Mill	Owner or Major Shareholder	% of Quota	% Accum.
1) Pantaleón	Herrera Ibargüen	16.3	16.3
2) Concepción	Witman	12.9	29.2
3) Santa Ana	Botrán	12.0	41.2
4) La Unión	Molina Calderón	9.1	50.3
5) Palo Gordo	Luis González Bauer	7.5	57.8
6) Madre Tierra	Campollo López	6.8	64.6
7) El Pilar	Weissenber Campollo	6.0	70.6
8) El Salto	Alejos	5.1	75.7
9) Tierra Buena	García Granados	4.3	80.0
10) El Baúl	Herrera	4.1	84.1

Note: The remaining ten mills are Los Tarros, San Diego, Guadalupe, Tululá, Magdalena, Santa Teresa, Trinidad, Mirandilla, San Antonio and La Sonrisa, which together produce the remaining 15.9 per cent of the sugar quota. At least 13 of the mills are situated in the department of Escuintla, where around three-quarters of sugar cultivation takes place.

commercial or industrial interests linked to sugar production. As in El Salvador, where three mills control two-thirds of production, a small number of *ingenios* process the majority of Guatemala's sugar cane. In 1983 the largest four mills (Pantaleón, Concepción, Santa Ana and La Unión) controlled half of the country's sugar production, while the top ten controlled 84 per cent (see table above). Pantaleón and Concepción account for around two-thirds of total sugar exports.[31]

Roberto Herrera Ibárgüen is the owner of the largest mill at Pantaleón, which is run by the Pantaleón Sugar Company, with net assets of US$36 million.[32] He has an English wife and studied in London. He is also a leading member of the Herrera family, who by repute are the second wealthiest family in Guatemala. The family had built their fortune on coffee in the 19th century, but although they still maintained some coffee, cotton and cattle-farming interests, the main base of their wealth had shifted to the cultivation, refining and marketing of sugar.[33] Roberto was a militant of the far-right National Liberation Movement (MLN) and Minister of the Interior under Arana in the early 1970s, and as such was one of the few members of the traditional Guatemalan oligarchy to have held public office. He broke with the MLN in the mid-1970s after challenging the iron grip maintained on the party by its antediluvian leader, Mario Sandoval Alarcón. In January 1978 he was kidnapped by the Guerrilla Army of the Poor (EGP) and released only after a ransom had been paid and a communiqué published detailing his involvement in repression.

Pat Goudvis

Cane-cutter on Pantaleón sugar plantation

A separate branch of the Herrera family, who own the company named Agrícola e Industrial El Baúl SA, control not only the mill at El Baúl in Escuintla but also 42 other plantations. On two of these, Rosario Canajal and San Antonio Sinaché (measuring a total of 11,400 acres) in southern Quiché, farm tenants as recently as 1976 were still allocated small plots of land in exchange for fixed periods of seasonal labour on the family's commercial farms. The extended family are believed to have interests, although not necessarily a controlling interest, in as many as six of the country's *ingenios*.

The name of García Granados features again as having a major interest in the Tierra Buena mill, which is owned by a company named Agroinsa SA. The small but oldest mill in Guatemala at Tululá is owned by the Bouscayrol family. They were identified by the North American Congress on Latin America (NACLA) as one of the key twenty families of the Guatemalan bourgeoisie who moved from commerce to land in the 19th century and at present have a wide range of industrial interests in addition to sugar refining.[34] Perhaps the most infamous name is that of Roberto Alejos, who owns the mill at El Salto situated in 12,000 acres of prime land in Escuintla. In total, Alejos owns between 20,000 and 25,000 acres of sugar cane, worth an estimated US$16 million at 1986 prices. Alejos' personal history is a rich mixture of personal gain and fierce opposition to local and international social change. In the early 1960s he was active in the struggle to overthrow Castro in the Bay of Pigs invasion:

> The Americans were secretly planning an invasion of Cuba to overthrow Fidel Castro and needed a base of operations on foreign soil. President Ydígoras agreed to cooperate, provided the US back him fully inside Guatemala. He persuaded conservative businessman Roberto Alejos, an old friend and associate, to turn over his plantation in the province of Retalhuleu to the Americans for use as an air base and training site. Alejos was a former employee of both the CIA and United Fruit and had been a confidant of Castillo Armas. He acted officially as President Ydígoras' link to foreign aid programs, a lucrative position for graft. His brother Carlos, Guatemala's ambassador to Washington, was Ydígoras' intermediary with the CIA in setting up the deal.[35]

In 1984 Alejos owned a spectacular country house in the hills above Guatemala City, at least three cars, and a helicopter with which to fly to visit his plantations. He employs 5,000-6,000 workers at harvest time but the last union to exist at El Salto was repressed and later disbanded after the death of twelve of its leaders in 1980. During an interview in a 1984 BBC TV documentary Alejos defined what he understood by the 'freedom' of his Indian workers: 'I'd like to see those Indians who are complaining that they are poor. I don't think there's a freer element in Guatemalan society than the Indians. They're not permanent employees to anyone. They come down to the coast to work for a time, to make some extra wages, then they go back to their own land where they have their own rights and their own freedoms.' Alejos has also been mentioned as a potential presidential candidate for the 1989 elections.

Another major sugar family are the Botráns, who own the Santa Ana sugar mill (which is also part-owned by exiled Cubans). The family cultivates sugar cane both for export and to produce their own famous brand of rum, *Ron Botrán*, in their factory in Quezaltenango. History has it that at the turn of the century five of the Botrán brothers arrived from Spain and started up a small distillery. From such small beginnings, the extended family expanded into industrial concerns including vodka production, transport, and stone-quarrying for making cement, and acquired a financial interest in the private development bank, FIASA, set up by USAID in 1969 to integrate US transnationals and local industrialists in joint operations.

In 1985 Alejandro Botrán was for a time the President of CACIF, and he is also head of the Sugar-Growers Association (ASAZGUA), which groups together the main sugar-growers and mill owners, and acts as the sole exporter for the sugar mills. ASAZGUA's members continued to do well in 1986 despite low international prices for sugar, worldwide overproduction and reduced US quotas for Guatemalan sugar. Because of the devaluation of the quetzal, exporters were receiving Q22.50 a quintal, roughly equivalent to the price in the official domestic market, which sugar producers described as 'highly profitable'.[36] The average consumer was the real loser because artificial shortages — largely created by wholesalers either waiting for a higher price or illegally shipping sugar to other Central American countries — had caused the price of sugar to double since 1984. When, in September 1986, sugar-growers were guaranteed a price of Q27 a ton for cut cane — almost double the guaranteed price of 1984-5 — it was too much for Alejandro Falla, the president of the Commission for Price Regulation. He resigned in protest at the government decision, arguing that 'it affected the most needy sectors of the country'.[37]

Beef Barons

No other agro-export has contributed less to the welfare of the Guatemalan population than beef. Cattle-ranching has displaced hundreds of small farmers and employed very few workers. Moreover, Guatemala was no exception to the process common throughout Central America by which the countries of the region rapidly increased beef exports to the US to meet the demands of the fast-food chains like MacDonalds, while per capita domestic consumption declined. Like sugar and cotton, the beef boom brought benefits to only a few large cattle-ranchers. Although there were more than 100,000 farm units raising cattle in 1979, a mere seven per cent of these possessed 70 per cent of the country's stock (see table, page 31). As one North American expert has written recently: 'for those with privileged access to the titling press and bank credit, the beef-export boom meant a quick way to expand family fortunes. For the millions of Central Americans who plant food crops for survival, it spelled doom.'[38]

It was only in the 1960s that beef ceased to be considered a non-traditional export. Backed by US$100 millions' worth of international assistance from the IDB, USAID and the World Bank and helped by the easing of US import restrictions under the Nixon administration, beef soon joined cotton and sugar as the third new and profitable agro-export. Meat exports rose from 0.1 per cent of all agricultural exports in 1960 to an average of 5 per cent in the 1970s, and reached the value of US$28 million in 1977.

The cattle boom began in Pacific departments like Retalhuleu and Escuintla, where cattle had been raised since the colonial period.

Starting in the 1960s new cattle-ranchers rapidly expanded into the north-eastern departments, and especially Zacapa, Izabal and the Petén. But where they moved in, they often clashed with or dispossessed long-resident Indian and *ladino* farmers or recent Indian migrants in resettlement zones in the Northern Transversal Strip. These conflicts were always potentially explosive because, unlike cotton and sugar, cattle could be raised almost anywhere, including the poor or marginal land which was also claimed by the poor farmers. Moreover, these rapidly-expanding cattle farms offered few jobs to evicted peasants because of their low labour requirements.

Two of the most bloody acts of army repression during counter-insurgency operations took place in cattle boom areas. Colonel Arana, the so-called 'Butcher of Zacapa' and President of Guatemala from 1970 to 1974, became one of the largest cattle-ranchers in North-East Guatemala after 'clearing' the area of at least 6,000 supposed guerrillas, many of whom were in fact peasants resisting land evictions, while the infamous massacre of more than one hundred Kekchí Indians in the town square at Panzós on 29 May 1978 stemmed from land conflicts between Indians and local expansionist cattle-ranchers. According to one report, the landowners actually fired the first shots that triggered the volley of fire from the army detachment and led to the ensuing mountain of Indian dead.[39] The Panzós massacre was possibly the single most important factor in bringing Indians into the armed struggle.[40]

Two of the best known and largest cattle ranchers on the south coast are Roberto Berger in Escuintla and Manuel Ralda. By repute, Ralda owns 42 *fincas* in Retalhuleu. Together with a third cattle-rancher and Cuban exile, Gerardo Sampedro, they set up a company named El Ganadero SA in 1962, which soon became one of the largest meat-packing and processing plants in the region, exporting industrial wax and animal feeds to the rest of Central America. In general, the owners of packing plants receive the greatest concentration of profits: preferential rights to the US market are issued to them, and the slaughtering of cattle and beef processing are the most profitable phases of the cattle business.[41]

The millionaire Juan Maegli, who describes himself as a 'public relations officer for Guatemala', provides an example of an aggressive businessman taking advantage of the cattle boom and quickly acquiring large cattle farms in the east of the country. Starting in the 1970s, Maegli bought up five *fincas* to the south of Lake Izabal — named El Chapín, Pataxte, Río Zarquito, Selempín and Chaviland — which together measured more than 4,500 hectares and were worth around Q3 million at 1986 prices. Although the *fincas* also produced wood and cardamom, Maegli's main concern was his estimated 60,000 head of cattle. His two aeroplanes allowed him to make regular visits to the *fincas* while living in Guatemala City, where he looked after a variety of business concerns including a company importing agricultural inputs (Tecún SA), and a department store and jewellery shop (both part of the Magno Group).

When Maegli moved onto the Río Zarquito *finca*, the 100-odd Kekchí families who originally lived on the area were slowly displaced from their land and joined the ranks of the non-resident workers on the farms. In 1983 Maegli allowed the army to resettle 30 refugee families from the mountains on the Selempín *finca*, whom he later used as cheap labour on his plantations. But in June 1986 he suddenly ordered them to leave the *finca* and go and join other refugees living on the public land on the shores of Lake Izabal. As one priest observed at the time: 'less than one hectare of land each would have been enough to sustain the families.'[42]

Generals Inc.

'Every military man who has occupied the Presidency since 1970,' wrote the Guatemala-based weekly *This Week* in July 1986, 'has ended his term a millionaire several times over.'[43] *This Week* might have added that it is not just ex-presidents but a high percentage of past and present Guatemalan generals who have joined the caste of military millionaires. The process by which the army became an economic power in its own right started in the 1960s when individual generals and colonels used their tenure of office to plunder the state's resources and thereby join Guatemala's wealthy elite. In the early 1970s the army as an institution established a substantial economic base through its interests in at least 40 semi-autonomous state enterprises. Top of the pile are the army's own bank (El Banco del Ejército) and the aptly-named Military Social Welfare Institute (Instituto de Previsión Militar or IPM). For generals to be rich and for a military institution to have some control over key sectors of the economy are not rare phenomena in Latin America, but the Guatemalan officer class has acquired an unparalleled notoriety for its corruption, voracity and entrepreneurial zeal. Most senior officers have an extensive stake in the country's economy and some argue that they are fighting to defend their own privileges as well as those of the *ladino* elite.

Successive military presidents have ensured a large executive budget and defence expenditure partly in order to grease their own palms and partly to buy the allegiance of their junior officers. Published figures show that the defence budget jumped from 10 per cent of total government expenditure in 1975 to 22 per cent in 1985, while in real terms it is considered to reach as much as a third of the national outlay.[44] Although the precise figures are classified, in 1986 the 21 colonels in command of regions were said to be earning between Q15,000 and Q18,000 a month each, of which between a third and a half was paid in US dollars (using the lower estimate, this was the approximate equivalent of US$8,500 or £6,000 a month), while the average private earned Q150 a month (approximately US$50 or £35).[45]

The defence budget is not just designed to pay salaries. According to the private-sector linked National Centre for Economic Research (CIEN), over half the total 1984 budget would have been lost to 'corruption, debt, squandering and confidential disbursements ... that are used to pay government-sponsored paramilitary groups and death squads, maintain clandestine jails, and bribe delegates, politicians, journalists, ex-triumvirates, union leaders, and one or another business leaders.'[46] The officer corps also enjoy privileged access to duty-free luxury imports like electrical goods and Scotch whisky through the army commissary, while BMWs and Mercedes are the norm for senior officers. Virtually free air travel abroad, generous petrol allowances, a luxury 800-unit housing complex in Santa Rosita and a retirement haven in Antigua are among additional comforts provided for the ruling brass.[47]

Such privileges are not as significant as the sheer diversity of economic interests and control that the army built up in the 1970s and 1980s. High-ranking military officials became big landowners and major shareholders in financial, industrial and commercial companies. The best known act of rapid wealth accumulation was the acquisition of vast domains in the Northern Transversal Strip (FTN) development zone by top military officers in the 1970s. Presidents Arana, Laugerud and Lucas were all said to have handed out properties to high and middle-ranking officers and their civilian collaborators, who were soon enjoying the rewards of cattle ranching, and rubber and *chicle* (chewing gum) production.[48] Extensive tracts of land originally designed for settlement by peasants from the overcrowded *altiplano* under the protection of INTA, were bought up by military officers. By 1979 *Newsweek* had already dubbed the area 'the Zone of the Generals'.

General Romeo Lucas García (Minister of Defence under Laugerud and President from 1978 to 1982) is the most notorious landowner, with at least 14,000 hectares in the Northern Transversal Strip including the 11,000-hectare Yalpemech *finca* owned jointly with Raúl

---

Military Economic Interests

At year-end 1985, the military had effective economic and managerial control over the following:

● AVIATECA, the national airline, whose planes are owned by the Guatemalan Air Force. In August 1984 highly-placed military employees were accused of authorising trips to the US for themselves and their wives for the symbolic fee of Q1.75 (US$.60 or 40 pence). AVIATECA has been described by the *Financial Times* as a 'cash-cow for military purposes'.

● TAM (Military Air Transport), which is a small business competing with other privately-owned air companies. TAM is accused of 'unfair competition' by its adversaries because of its access to military runways, cheap Air Force fuel, tax breaks, and state-funded maintenance.

● The main Aurora international airport.

● GUATEL, the public telecommunications system (used for counter-insurgency purposes).

● INDE, the state-owned electricity company.

● Channel 5 TV station, which broadcasts pro-military propaganda, along with educational programmes. The military are also said to have an interest in two privately-owned TV channels, 11 and 13.

● Two defence factories, one manufacturing munitions (M-16 and Galil Assault rifles) in Cobán, and the other armoured vehicles in Santa Ana Berlín, Coatepeque, Quezaltenango.

● The ports, the National Geographical Institute, CONE (the Disaster Relief Organisation), CRN (the Committee for National Reconstruction), FYDEP (the development agency for the Petén) and at least 20 other parastatal agencies mostly under the direction of the S-5 (the army's Civilian Affairs Unit). The most important of these are BANVI (National Housing Bank), DIGESA (Agricultural Services Agency) and INTECAP (Technical Training Institute).

García Granados. Other senior officers like General Arana (President from 1970 to 1974), Otto Spiegeler (Minister of Defence under Lucas), David Rubio Coronado (Minister of Defence under Laugerud) and Benedicto Lucas (brother of Romeo) are among those known to have extensive landed interests in the area. Precise figures are hard to come by because land is often held in the name of companies or third parties, but one recent study completed by a team of Jesuits estimated that four former government functionaries owned 285,000 hectares here, while a 1983 AID-financed study claimed that 60 per cent of the department of Alta Verapaz was owned by the army.[49]

More important politically than this relatively small group of landed generals is the plethora of state or semi-state organisations which are run or controlled by the army (see box, page 49). The most important of these, the IPM, masquerades as a pension and investment fund for the military but is more accurately described as a tax-free business corporation whose profits find their way into the pockets of senior military officers. Amongst the IPM's many economic concerns are the army commissary, an insurance company, a multi-storey car park in Guatemala City, and several urban properties. Under Lucas, IPM money was going to be used in consort with South African finance to build a large US$100m cement factory with a virtual monopoly over the supply of concrete to huge government infrastructure projects (thereby stepping on the toes of the Novella family's monopoly over cement production), but the deal fell through when Lucas declined to guarantee credits.[50]

IPM's biggest concern is the Bank of the Army (El Banco del Ejército), which it set up in 1972 with the help of appropriated public funds and which now counts military officers among its major shareholders. The bank, whose advertising slogan describes it with multiple irony as 'the safest place for your money', has lent money for the development of cattle-raising and other agro-exports, industry and real estate, but it is also 'notorious for its flagrant corruption'.[51] By 1985 it had become the seventh largest bank in Guatemala, with total assets of Q185 million, overtaking more established banks like Lloyds International and the Banco del Agro.

Military control over state enterprises is said to have allowed senior officers to amass considerable personal fortunes. Nowhere was the bureaucratisation of large-scale corruption more evident than in a series of large public works projects initiated under Lucas. Hydro-electric dams, ports and highways provided the easiest source of gain through kickbacks and commissions. These projects also became the target of constant criticism by the private sector for their contribution to the country's national debt and inflated fiscal deficit. CACIF's pet hate was the graft-plagued Chixoy hydro-electric dam, which was originally designed to reduce Guatemala's dependence on imported oil. Because of construction defects the project has not worked properly since it was completed in 1982, and in the meantime the cost spiralled from US$360 million at conception to over US$900 million by late 1985, a large part of which was believed to be the result of misappropriation of funds. When another of these huge military-sponsored infrastructure projects, the Puerto Quetzal port in Escuintla, was finally opened in November 1985, it had overshot its budget by more than US$100 million.

The story goes that the system of corruption changed under the regime of Ríos Montt because of his insistence on honesty and his emphasis on cutting the fiscal deficit and channelling more funds towards the war effort. This prompted a different form of military self-enrichment amongst a new clique of generals, which was rumoured to include Mejía Víctores (President 1983-1986), Lobos Zamora (Mejía's Chief of Staff), Edilberto Letona (head of the Mariscal Zavala base in Guatemala City), Jaime Hernández (former head of the Guard of Honour and first Minister of Defence under Cerezo), and Héctor Gramajo (second Minister of Defence under Cerezo). These and other generals were said to have made sizeable profits by dollar speculation on the black market. The system was simple: they would acquire dollars at the Q1:US$1 rate through the Bank of Guatemala or the Bank of the Army and then change the dollars back into quetzals at the Q3:US$1 rate through the foreign exchange houses they controlled.[52]

Lobos Zamora — who is also said to be a major cattle and drug smuggler — was widely rumoured to have used the profits from such dealings to help him become a major shareholder (along with the then Foreign Minister, Fernando Andrade) in one of Guatemala's newest banks, the Banco del Quetzal.[53] In 1984 Mejía had to make an embarrassing public denial of his involvement in any illegal dollar dealing when a woman named Eugenia Bufalino, who was said to be his mistress, was discovered at Miami airport to have US$30 million amongst her luggage. The only drawback to such lucrative dollar dealings was that they were based in Guatemala City and are believed to have provoked serious murmurings of discontent amongst younger regional commanders. Rumour has it that these soon died down after the colonels had received presents of US$5,000 and Q5,000 a month, free trips abroad and even luxury cars.[54]

Big Business

In the cases of coffee, cotton, sugar and beef, it is the Guatemalan agrarian elite which owns the land on which the agro-exports are grown. US transnationals usually monoplise the external marketing and trading arms of the business. All branches of the banana business, however, are dominated by one US transnational, Del Monte. The company started operations in 1972 when it acquired United Fruit's banana interests for US$20 million, allegedly after a US$500,000 bribe paid by Del Monte to a close associate of the then President, Carlos Arana, to secure the deal.[55] Del Monte is a subsidiary of R.J. Reynolds, the largest consumer products corporation in the world, whose global interests include Winston and

Camel cigarettes and Nabisco products. Although for the company Guatemala represents only a minor financial concern, it is the country's single largest private employer (of 5,500 workers). In the 1970s Bandegua, Del Monte's subsidiary in Guatemala, owned or controlled 55,000 acres of highly productive plantation land in the hot tropical lowlands of north-eastern Guatemala. But of these 55,000, only 9,000 acres were actually under cultivation, while the total area growing bananas in the 1970s amounted on average to 12,500 acres a year.

However, it is not in the production but in the marketing of bananas where the most money is to be made. More than 80 per cent of the final price paid by the high-street shopper is estimated to be captured by the various stages of trading and marketing bananas, all controlled by transnationals.[56] The three giant banana companies, Del Monte, Castle and Cooke and United Brands, together account for 60 per cent of the world's banana market and 90 per cent of the US market. Moreover, in Guatemala Bandegua totally monopolises the cleaning, packing and transportation of the country's bananas, whereas in Ecuador, Colombia and Nicaragua, national companies control 100 per cent of the local end of the marketing process.

In addition, Del Monte has succeeded in persuading recent military governments to reduce taxes by arguing the need to maintain competitive advantage (over other transnationals) and threatening to reduce production or pull out altogether. As of 1986, Bandegua enjoyed export sales of around US$60 million but paid no taxes on the boxes of bananas it exported, in contrast to the taxes imposed by all the other Central American banana-producing countries and despite the aim of taxing bananas at US$1 per box agreed by the Union of Banana Exporting Countries (UPEB) in 1974. In February 1985, with the help of President Reagan's then roving ambassador, Richard Stone, Bandegua also negotiated a special deal with the Mejía government for a loan of US$30 million for necessary imports after threatening to withdraw from Guatemala. One recent study summarised Bandegua's role in Guatemala:

> Bandegua is allied with the most reactionary elements within the Guatemalan bourgeoisie; it manipulates workers to avoid labour unrest; and together with other banana companies, it has tried to torpedo efforts by Central American governments to gain greater control over their natural resources [...] Del Monte reinforces economic underdevelopment and political reaction in Guatemala, and acts as a formidable obstacle to change.[57]

Bananas are no longer the major transnational interest in

Guatemala. Starting in the 1960s, US (and European) transnationals have moved into the manufacturing, agribusiness, banking, service and petroleum sectors. Many transnational executives have become part of the local power structure through their privileged access to military and government officials, their links to US economic and political agencies, and their powerful lobby organisations like the American Chamber of Commerce and *Amigos del País*. Some officials of such organisations are notorious for their militant defence of the 'need' for death squads or human rights violations 'in order to beat the guerrillas'.[58] Three transnationals are also among those with the worst record for anti-union violence: Coca-Cola (12 killed), the meat-packing firm Prokesa (six killed) and Warner Lambert, whose subsidiary Adams Products makes chewing gum and health-care products (at least one killed).

In 1985, 483 branches, affiliates or subsidiaries of US transnationals were operating in Guatemala, including 90 of the top 500 US companies (which gave Guatemala the largest transnational presence in Central America except Panama), with direct investments of between US$200 and US$400 million.[59] Transnational investment far outweighs national industrial capital, and in the early 1980s it represented 27 per cent of total investment, the highest percentage in Latin America.[60] Part of the reason for this is that successive military governments have ensured a favourable investment climate for these firms by tax exemptions and generous profit repatriation. For example, legislation passed in 1975 provided for a 100 per cent tax exemption on profits for five years, and a one-year exemption from import taxes on various industrial inputs.[61]

The transnationals began to invest substantially in the industrial sector with the development of the Central American Common Market (CACM) in the 1960s. Immediately after the 1954 coup, Guatemala became a US-directed 'showcase for development' in which the chosen method of proving the merits of a 'free' country over the 'communist' Arbenz regime was a rapid influx of economic aid. This amounted to between US$80 and US$90 million — more than the entire funding for the rest of Latin America — which was accompanied by a sevenfold increase in the number of aid personnel to administer it.[62] But the failure of this strategy (largely due to simple corruption) was one of the main reasons for the impetus given by US-controlled banks and development agencies to the CACM. The purpose of the CACM was to reduce the region's dependence on cash crops and develop an industrial sector. This was to be achieved, not by expanding each country's domestic market (through a land reform or income redistribution as under Arbenz), but by integrating the regional

---

The Guatemalan Rockefellers

The Castillos are the richest and most dynamic family of Guatemala and they dominate the industrial sector. Starting with a small beer factory at the end of the 19th century, the various branches of the extended family have diversified into soft drinks, milk and beef production, glass manufacture, soft drinks distribution, and property and investment companies. 1986 marked the centenary of the foundation of their first beer company, Cervecería Centroamericana SA. One hundred years of 'believing, trusting and investing in Guatemala' has brought the family total estimated assets of Q400 million, equivalent to 31 per cent of the 1985 national budget.

Despite the variety of economic interests, the family's monopoly of beer production remains their principal source of wealth. The two brothers, Mariano and Rafael Castillo Córdova, founded Cervecería Centroamericana SA back in 1886, and the company still operates today with two factories in Guatemala City and one in Quezaltenango, producing (amongst others) the two most popular brands of beer, Gallo and Monte Carlo. Ever since the Castillos acquired Cervecería Nacional SA in Quezaltenango in 1929, owned by their then fiercest rivals, the Keine brothers, they have remained the only beer producers in the country. In 1940 the company started to produce Canada Dry drinks under licence, and later in 1947 a separate subsidiary, Embotelladora Salvavidas SA, was set up to directly produce Canada Dry, Orange Crush, Lemon Crush and distilled water. In 1957 they formed Central Distribuidora SA in Guatemala City to market all the company's products — by 1986 their publicity boasted that nine out of every ten shops in Guatemala stocked products supplied by Central Distribuidora. In the early 1960s they also set up their own publicity firm Mercomún Publicidad SA to advertise the company's goods.

Cervecería Centroamericana is the eleventh largest company in Guatemala with assets worth US$78 million. The company also has extensive interests in milk and cattle production on their *finca* Agua Tibia in San José Pinula in the department of Guatemala; it has an estimated 20 per cent interest in the glass manufacturing company ▶

---

consumer market of all Central America's upper and middle classes and protecting it for locally manufactured goods by a series of external tariffs to keep out foreign manufacturers.

However, largely as a result of the relaxation of restrictions on foreign investment and the failure of the regional planning and financial institutions to protect local investors, transnationals came to dominate and control both the regional market for manufactured goods and Guatemala's rapidly expanding manufacturing sector. They

CAVISA, the tenth largest company, with assets of US$95 million; and another of its subsidiaries, Alimentos SA, produces and markets Incaparina, the high-protein milk substitute devised by INCAP for low-income families. Another member of the original Castillo Córdova family, Enrique, founded the bottling company La Mariposa in 1893, which now manufactures and distributes Pepsi-Cola, mineral water and fruit drinks. In 1957 a subsidiary company, Embotelladora del Pacífico was set up in Mazatenango, Suchitepéquez to serve the south coast and west of the country. A third branch of the family owns the popular radio station, Radio Ciros.

Over the years the Castillos have consolidated their wealth and position by intermarrying with other key Guatemalan families like the Fallas, Arenales, Aycinenas, Cofinos, Dorions, Sinibaldis and Toriellos. While some members of their clan are employed as managers of their various companies, others have become professionals, academics or occasionally government officials. At present the chief (or most visible) representatives of the family are: **Ramiro Castillo Love**, President of the Banco Industrial, the largest bank in Guatemala, with capital of Q390 million in 1985; **Edgar Castillo Sinibaldi**, chief representative of the Cervecería; **Jorge Castillo Love**, an economist and chief investor for the family. In 1970 he was first vice-President of FIASA, the USAID-funded investment bank set up in 1969, in which the Castillos were the principal shareholders and major beneficiaries; and **Alvaro Castillo Monge**, head of CACIF and the Cámara de Industria in 1986.

Surprisingly, only one member of the Castillo family, Dr. Raúl Castillo Love (an ex-dean of the faculty of dentistry in USAC) is known to have been kidnapped, and this was thought to be by the right. Despite the enormous potential rewards, no Castillo is known to have been kidnapped by the left. This may be because they are not known as accomplices of repression (unlike other rich families), or because they are said to 'collaborate' with groups or parties of all political persuasions. In addition, they have the reputation (at least in their beer factories) of paying their workers better than most other employers and offering substantial fringe benefits such as housing, health care and schooling.

partially or wholly acquired local companies (of the top 39 US companies which established manufacturing operations in the 1960s, 18 did so by buying out local firms), or they set up joint ventures with local businessmen, or they made production arrangements with competing firms. For example, in the food processing sector, a number of giant US companies like General Mills, Pillsbury, Ralston Purina, Central Soya, Coca-Cola, CPC International, Beatrice Foods, and Foremost-McKesson bought up local firms in the 1960s and thereby gained control of the processed food supply for most of Central America. These food companies are still active in Guatemala today. A similar process occurred in the key pharmaceutical and chemical industries as major transnationals stepped in to use Guatemala as a base for their regional operations.

Just as the Liberal Revolution had created the coffee oligarchy, the CACM bred a small Guatemalan industrial elite which for the most part functioned as a junior partner and ally of the transnationals. However, some important trading and manufacturing sectors are still entirely controlled by single Guatemalan families: the Castillos, the so-called 'Rockefellers of Guatemala', are the wealthiest family in Guatemala largely as a result of their monopoly of the country's beer production (see box, pages 54-5); the Novella family controls most of Guatemala's cement production through their company Cementos Progreso, the fifth largest company in Guatemala, with assets worth US$88 million; the Lamport family are one of the country's major importers (enjoying a monopoly in Johnnie Walker whisky); the Kongs (and especially the multimillionaire Jorge Kong) are said to be the most powerful family within the more corrupt business mafia, with a wide variety of economic interests which include a virtual monopoly of commercial soap and detergents, a cotton gin, cooking oil, and (formerly) with Milton Molina, control over flour production.

The CACM ran out of steam in the early 1970s mainly as a result of regional imbalances, market saturation, and the 1969 'soccer war' between Honduras and El Salvador. A new series of economic activities was promoted by the US aid agencies, including cattle-ranching, tourism, and new agribusiness projects like cut flowers, frozen fruit and vegetables, and latterly the high-yield crop cardamom (of which Guatemala is now the world's main producer). Smaller US 'sunbelt investors' were particularly attracted, and their interests once again lay not in the growth of a domestic market (for which domestic reforms would have been necessary) but in using Guatemala merely as a base of operations for the US market.

For example, Guatemala became the centre of operations for the USAID-financed LAAD (Latin American Agribusiness Development Corporation). This was founded in 1970 by a consortium of 15 mainly agribusiness transnationals, pulled together by the Bank of America, to develop non-traditional agro-exports. By the mid-1980s, there were over 60 LAAD-financed businesses in Guatemala, the most important of which was ALCOSA, a subsidiary of Hanover Brands, which processes and freezes vegetables like broccoli and cauliflower for the US market. USAID funds a number of projects to persuade small Indian producers to grow new export crops for

ALCOSA and other US companies, when such crops are known to displace Indian staple crops, and to involve more risks and expenses than traditional farming.[63]

The economic recession in the early 1980s caused more than 400 industrial establishments to close down. Of the remaining 1,910 firms, only 237, usually transnational-owned, employ more than 50 workers. At least 10,000 industrial workers lost their jobs. By 1985 industrial production had fallen to 14.6 per cent of GDP, and employed 12 per cent of the working population. However, there were few publicised cases of transnationals pulling out of the country. For example, in the chemicals sector, all the top ten US chemical companies (with interests mainly in the manufacturing and distribution of pesticides) still maintained their operations. In the service sector seven of the top eight US accounting firms had offices in Guatemala, while in the pharmaceutical sector 17 of the top 20 US companies were still active in the country, and reported to be enjoying profit margins of up to 300 per cent on some of their products in 1985.[64]

Transnationals remain the third colossus of the Guatemalan economy. Along with the generals and the family-based private sector, they have been the principal beneficiaries of the last 30 years of economic growth. Together they have turned an entire country into a limited company. The rewards from the boom in agro-exports have gone mainly into the pockets of the small number of families and transnationals who grow the crops and control the marketing. The army has been transformed from a guardian of the elite's wealth into a member of their club (and at times a potential competitor). The US-directed industrialisation and 'development' policies have not touched the monopoly of land and riches nor upset existing power groups, but on the contrary have brought the most benefits to transnationals and their local allies. The lack of social reforms has meant that the private sector continues to control the economy, in the words of the Economist Intelligence Unit, 'to an extent unparalleled anywhere in the region'.[65] Does the Christian Democrat party of the 1980s offer any hope of such reforms?

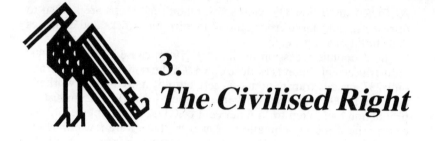

3.
The Civilised Right

'The key factor in the creation of a new order lies in the taking of power by the army and the Christian Democrat Party.' Vinicio Cerezo, 1977.

When Vinicio Cerezo and the Christian Democrat Party (DCG) scored a resounding victory in the 1985 elections, it was the first time that Guatemala had a Christian Democrat President or a Congress dominated by Christian Democrat representatives. But even before Vinicio donned the presidential sash, the prospects of his government being able to offer hope to the poor seemed remote. Partly this was due to the constraints set by the political process that had led to the elections, which will be described in the next chapter. But the grim outlook for the poor also stemmed from the origins, ideology and recent history of the Christian Democrat Party itself.

Ever since its foundation in 1955, the DCG has been profoundly 'anti-communist'. This 'anti-communism' does not mean simply opposition to the small and heavily-repressed Guatemalan Labour Party (PGT) (also known as the Communist Party), but includes a strong enmity towards popular, revolutionary or socialist movements both in Guatemala and in the rest of Latin America. In common with most other Christian Democrat parties in Latin America, the social reforms that the DCG has at times advocated are justified as 'a better way to fight communism' than the hardline options offered by more right-wing parties. There is a constant tension in all Christian Democrat parties between their deep-rooted anti-communism and the feasibility or desirability of reforms. But history has shown that under pressure the tension has always been resolved in favour of the former with the result that Christian Democrat parties in the final analysis stand by the dominant power groups in Latin America.

This is illustrated by the period of acute social polarisation in Guatemala that started in the mid-1970s. Hopelessly looking for a middle ground that did not exist, the DCG in effect sided with the rich and the right-wing parties and not with the poor and popular organisations. Despite periods of heavy repression of party members (especially under Lucas García), the party has observed a time-honoured tradition of allegiance to the electoral path as a method of bringing change to the country. This faith in 'legality' has left the party with a sorry record of participating in a series of electoral frauds and military-dominated Congresses which have served only to legitimise brutal military governments, and not to introduce a single substantive social reform.

Moreover, although in the 1960s and early 1970s the DCG was definitely a reforming centrist party, since 1974 it has survived by constantly shifting its politics and programme to the right. By the time of the 1985 elections, policies such as land reform, tax reform, or any state control of the trading or banking sector had been firmly rejected, and the DCG was left with a profile to the right of the Honduran Christian Democrat party or Napoleón Duarte's party in El Salvador. Despite the moderate image that Vinicio Cerezo or other Christian Democrat politicians adopted for local or foreign consumption, the party undoubtedly represented the 'civilised right'.

What is Christian Democracy?

Christian Democracy is probably best known because of the present-day strength of European Christian Democrat parties in West Germany, Italy, Holland and Belgium. Typically, European Christian Democrat parties were founded as a strongly pro-capitalist and anti-communist alternative to social-democrat and socialist parties in the reconstruction of Europe after the Second World War. Drawing on the European Catholic tradition and enjoying the support of important industrial and economic groups, they soon became the dominant conservative political parties in many countries of Western Europe.

The central body of Christian Democrat thinking springs from the social doctrine of the Catholic Church. This was first systematically expounded at the end of the 19th century in the encyclical of Pope Leo XIII, *Rerum Novarum*, in which the Pope criticised the abuses of liberal capitalism but also condemned socialism. He supported the social obligations of private property, and proposed a system of 'distributive justice' which would bring together or conciliate social classes, which he denied were in structural conflict with one another.

The idea of including Christian solutions to social problems was further developed by Pope Leo's successors: Pope Pius XI attacked the effects of laissez-faire capitalism and defended the workers' rights to organise, while Pope Pius XII (1939-58) encouraged the study of social sciences and the formation of Christian trade unions and Catholic Action groups, again to meet the challenge of strong communist movements in Western Europe.

The anti-communist bias of the Catholic position was softened by Pope John XXIII (1958-63), who distinguished between formal ideological positions and the groups who espoused them, and encouraged Catholics to collaborate with the adherents of other ideologies where this was for the common good. This pragmatism was reinforced by the Second Vatican Council (1962-65), which in particular recognised that Catholic responses could evolve to meet the needs of different historical periods and different situations, and moved away from the idea that there was invariably a 'Christian' solution to technical political and economic problems or any universal Christian model of social organisation. These developments legitimised the social involvement of radical Christians in Latin America, which later gave rise to the theology of liberation. The resulting formulations of Catholic social teaching were an uneasy compromise between the older bias towards conciliation and the new 'option for the poor', and different elements were used by different factions to support their position. The 'liberationist' strand was developed by two influential meetings of the Latin American bishops at Medellín (1968) and Puebla (1979), but remained under constant attack from conservative clergy and laity. Latin American Christian Democrat parties were generally to be found in the conservative camp.

Christian Democrat parties first appeared in Latin America in the 1950s and 1960s, and were closely linked financially and ideologically to their sister parties in Europe. Although Christian Democrat ideology is neither clear-cut nor consistent, as each party has adapted to the particular conditions of each country, most Latin American Christian Democrat parties resolve the apparent contradiction between individualism and the common good by espousing a loose 'communitarian' ideology which is neither capitalism nor communism. As Alfonso Cabrera, the present Secretary General of the Guatemalan Christian Democrat Party, has recently explained it, 'the principal objective of Christian Democrat parties is the establishment of a communitarianism in which individuals can be fulfilled through personalism and the common good, and which presents itself as an alternative between capitalism and communism.'[1] In practice, however, Christian Democrat reforms are generally kept firmly within the orbit of capitalism, albeit a more modernising version of it.

Much of the Christian Democrat ideology is underpinned by the religious or metaphysical tenet that the individual is the most important element in society. His or her individuality must be respected as well as his or her 'natural' rights, which include the right to private property. But at the same time society is the medium through which the individual has to develop both spiritually and materially, so society must be made to work for the common good. This means, for example, that although private property is seen as an absolute right, it should be used in a socially useful manner.

An equally important and fundamental Christian Democrat doctrine is the view that the interests of all sectors of society can and should be harmonised, which sharply distinguishes it from Marxist thought. Moreover, the Christian Democrats' faith in the possibility of love, peace and consensus between all social groups leads them fiercely to reject any political party or movement that promotes what they view as hatred between classes. This is seen as tantamount to rising up against God and Nature, and as such to be firmly opposed.

In contrast, Marxists would maintain that there are irreconcilable differences between social classes: expressed simply, in a free-market economy the owners of capital have to compete with other capitalists and do at least as well — otherwise they will ultimately fail and go bankrupt. In order to compete successfully, they have to keep production costs down as low as possible, which is not in the interests of those who sell their labour, whose well-being will always be subordinate to the exigencies of the market. This would also help to explain why the rich will not surrender their wealth, land or privileges without a fight, and why it is therefore fruitless to suppose that they would. Liberation theologians usually agree with Marxists in criticising any religious expression that makes 'lyrical calls to social harmony', arguing that for the church to ignore the fact of class conflict is equivalent to tacitly supporting a system that perpetuates the privileges of the few.[2] They would also maintain that sin lies as much in society and its unjust structures as in the individual, and so those structures must be changed for the salvation of all, both rich and poor.

Christian Democracy in Latin America

Christian Democracy burst on to the Latin American political map in the 1960s, first with the government of President Frei in Chile (1964-1970), and later with the victory of Dr. Rafael Caldera as leader of COPEI, the more conservative Venezuelan Christian Democrat Party (1969-1974). COPEI remains the largest and most influential Christian Democrat party in Latin America through the financial and political support it is able to give to the smaller Christian Democrat parties, especially in Central America. However, the best-known experiences of Christian Democracy are those of Frei's 'revolution in liberty' and, more recently , President Duarte's precarious rule in El Salvador from March 1984. In both governments the tension between the more modernising, populist or reformist strand of Christian Democrat thought and their trenchant anti-communism is very evident.

Frei received large infusions of US economic aid as part of the US-backed Alliance for Progress, which aimed to pre-empt more Cuban-style revolutions by implementing 'reforms from above'. A modernising programme was introduced that included an enlarged role for the state, progressive tax changes and an agrarian reform that expropriated inefficient land, in an attempt to tackle the country's problems within a capitalist framework and undercut the support for the powerful Chilean socialist and communist parties. Although the agrarian reform brought improvements to some peasant sectors, Frei's experiment ultimately failed to improve most workers' living standards or fundamentally alter Chile's inequitable social structures. Caught between its populist rhetoric and its fear of deepening the reforms, the Christian Democrat Party eventually split into three. Two smaller factions joined the left-wing Popular Unity government of Salvador Allende (1970-73), while the leadership and bulk of the party eventually opted for the counter-revolution. On 22 August 1973 the party openly called on the Chilean armed forces to take action against the democratically elected Popular Unity government. On 12 September — just one day after a coup which cost the lives of at least 20,000 Chileans — it sent an official message of congratulation to the military.

Although the parallels should not be pushed too far, the recent experience of the Duarte government in El Salvador shows some similarities with that of President Frei. By the time of his election victory in March 1984, Duarte represented a right-wing Christian Democrat Party as most of the left wing had split to join the broad left-wing coalition of the FDR-FMLN. Secondly, Duarte had become the key tool of the US government and the Salvadorean military in pre-empting more radical change and undercutting support for the FDR-FMLN. To that end, since coming to office Duarte has received around US$2 million a day of economic and military aid from the Reagan administration, and he depends on this money. In addition, the trade union grouping funded by the American Institute for Free Labor Development (AIFLD), the Popular Democratic Unity, had been set up by the US as a means of giving Duarte a popular base to counteract the appeal of the FMLN. But by early 1987, Duarte's failure to fulfil his mandate for internal reform and a negotiated settlement to the war meant that his government was merely legitimising counter-insurgency.

It is hard not to conclude that, whether out of ideological conviction, an exaggerated fear of communism, or political opportunism, Latin American Christian Democrat parties have ultimately worked to the advantage of the US and their countries' dominant power groups and have not reduced social polarisation. Nor have they brought lasting solutions to the poverty of the majority.

The Quest for the Third Way

Throughout the 30 years of its existence the Guatemalan Christian Democrat Party has trodden a similar zigzag path between reforms and anti-communism. Its roots are deeply conservative. It was formed essentially as a strongly Christian, but still solidly anti-communist, response to the Arbenz experience of 1950-1954. Colonel Arbenz had followed a path of reforms aimed at modernising the country's economy along essentially capitalist lines. But at the height of the Cold War period the Eisenhower administration was unduly alarmed by the influence of the Guatemalan Communist Party (the PGT) within the Arbenz government and by Arbenz's independent foreign policy. Spurred on by the United Fruit Company, which stood to lose vast tracts of land under Arbenz's agrarian reform, in 1953 Eisenhower authorised the CIA to orchestrate Arbenz's overthrow. In a remarkable foretaste of present-day Reagan administration policies on Nicaragua, the democratically elected Arbenz was brought down by a group of mercenaries led by Colonel Castillo Armas in the name of 'saving the region from Soviet domination'. The early Christian Democrats unequivocally supported the counter-revolution. The first Christian Democrat leaders dedicated a plaque to Castillo Armas as the 'liberator of his country'.

Although there had been attempts in the early 1950s to set up an anti-Arbenz Social Christian Party under the inspiration of small Christian study groups, the Christian Democrat Party was not formally founded until 24 August 1955. Its membership was essentially drawn from middle class professionals, Catholic Action groups and members of rich agrarian families like the Herrartes and Cofiños.[3] It also received the initial support of the Archbishop of Guatemala, Monsignor Mariano Rosell Arellano, who had played a key role in mobilising support against Arbenz, and even on one occasion referred to Castillo Armas as a 'legitimate saint'. From its inception the Christian Democrat Party projected itself as a third alternative to the reforms of Arbenz and the rabid right-wing fanaticism of parties like Castillo Armas' National Democrat Movement (MDN), the predecessor of the better-known and self-proclaimed 'party of organised violence', the MLN (National Liberation Movement).

The first presidential elections the Christian Democrats contested in 1957 set the pattern for later years. The elections were largely designed to prove the 'democratic' nature of post-Arbenz Guatemala. They were fraudulent, and in the re-run the Christian Democrats showed their willingness to work closely with the far right. The party put up as its candidate Miguel Asturias Quiñónez, later to be a co-founder of the Granai and Thomson bank. Asturias' position as former Minister of Education under Armas helped convince any doubters of his anti-communist pedigree, while his platform was essentially that of fighting communism through applying vague notions of 'social justice'. However, in the re-run of the elections in February 1958, the Christian Democrats joined in a grand anti-communist alliance and supported the candidature of Colonel José Luis Cruz Salazar, allegedly after a payment had been made by the CIA to the party to drop its original candidate.[4]

In the early 1960s the party began to adopt more progressive or developmentalist positions, and slowly built up widespread support amongst students, *campesinos* and trade unions. With financial support from USAID through the Alliance for Progress, and some organisational and ideological overlap with the social work of the church, Indian peasant farmers and workers were encouraged to form cooperatives or Christian-orientated trade unions. Research institutes like IDESAC and the School of Cooperativism were also set up as Christian Democrat spin-offs. More significant in the early years was the growing Christian Democrat influence in the student movement through the Jesuit-directed Central American University Youth, and later FESC (the Social Christian Student Front). FESC provided the initial orientation for key political figures in the 1980s like Vinicio Cerezo, Fernando Andrade, Jorge Serrano Elías, and Danilo Barillas. The younger party activists were less imbued with the anti-communism of the older leaders, and helped to influence the party towards more reformist positions.

The shift was aided by a split in the party in 1964 when one faction of more recalcitrant anti-communists under Dr. Uclés wanted to go along with the 1963 Peralta military coup and accept ten seats in Congress. While Uclés left to become a founding member of the Democratic Institutional Party (PID) — whose basic function was to act as an electoral vehicle for senior military officers — the rest of the party leadership identified more with popular interests through the peasant union FCG, the union grouping in FECETRAG, and the shanty-town dwellers organisation MONAP, all of which were promoted as virtual parallel popular organisations for the party. The party's more progressive position was confirmed by its electoral platform for the 1970 elections, which it contested in alliance with a number of smaller social-democrat groupings. Their candidate, Major Lucas Caballeros — an economist and professor at USAC — even went so far as to reject the gradualism of the rival Revolutionary Party (PR)'s programme, which 'wouldn't guarantee our peasants land until the year 2100, when other men will be cultivating the Moon and Mars', and promised instead a complete and rapid agrarian reform.[5]

To many observers, and to many Christian Democrat supporters, 1974 was the watershed for the party. It marked the high point in the party's popularity, which coincided with its most radical blueprint for changing Guatemalan society. The 'Plan for Government 1974-1978' was highly critical of the private sector for 'maintaining a situation of exploitation, economic stagnation, destitution and social violence', which it hoped to rectify by a programme of agrarian reform, the promotion of an industrial base, the implementation of a minimum salary, an expansion of the internal market, and state participation in the economy. Despite the radical nature of its programme (which history would later show was tantamount to demanding a revolution) the same 'Plan for Government' still described the Christian Democrat position as promoting a 'personalist and communitarian society' as a third way between capitalism and socialism.[6]

In the 1974 elections the Christian Democrats joined an alliance with the social-democrat parties, the FUR and PRA, to form the powerful National Opposition Front (FNO). General Ríos Montt was chosen as the FNO's candidate, not because he shared all their views but because his reputed honesty represented the best hope of preventing the military from denying the coalition its possible victory. In the event Ríos Montt was not a sufficient guarantee: the FNO was widely considered to have won the vote, but not the count. The FNO claimed between 45 and 49 per cent of the vote to the 34 per cent gained by MLN-PID's candidate, General Kjell Laugerud. Clearly influenced by the threat made by the outgoing President, General Arana, that he would employ 'all the might that goes with holding power' to ensure Laugerud's triumph, the military emerged from three days' internal haggling to impose Laugerud.[7] After a private talk with Arana, Ríos Montt chose exile for himself and unity for the army, rather than reforms for the country. He was later quietly shipped off to Spain as military attaché.

The Quest for Government

The ten years after Ríos Montt's capitulation are central to

The Christian Democrats' Road to Government

1955: The party is founded on 24 August 1955 with 5,634 members. In December forms pact with ultra-right-wing parties such as the National Democrat Movement (MDN) and the Anti-Communist Unification Party (PUA), to contest Congressional elections.

1957: Contests presidential elections for first time in October, with candidature of Miguel Asturias Quiñónez, Minister of Education under Castillo Armas.

1958: In re-run of fraudulent presidential elections in February joins alliance that includes PUA and MDN, and led by Colonel Cruz Salazar.

1964: Party splits over whether to support 1963 coup by General Peralta, one group joining the party of senior military officers, the Democratic Institutional Party (PID).

1966: Does not fight elections after registration is blocked.

1967: Party re-registers during administration of Méndez Montenegro.

1970: Contests election under candidature of retired Major Lucas Caballero on a ticket that includes moderate reforms and the participation of smaller social-democrat parties. Comes third with 20 per cent of the vote and wins four seats in Congress.

1974: Contests fraudulent presidential elections with candidature of General Ríos Montt as member of the National Opposition Front (FNO), which includes two social-democrat parties, and puts forward the party's most radical programme. The FNO is widely believed to win the popular vote, but not the count. Ríos Montt backs down from confrontation with the military. The party accepts 15 seats in Congress.

1978: Contests fraudulent 1978 presidential elections with General ▶

---

understanding the nature of the Christian Democrat Party in the mid-1980s. Despite the 1974 experience the party was prepared to contest the next two fraudulent generals' elections of 1978 and 1982, which served only to keep in power illegal and repressive military regimes. This faith in the electoral path was one of the factors that caused the party slowly to lose its more left-wing activists. It progressively became a top-heavy party headed by a right-wing and opportunistic leadership rather than a party with a broadly-based membership and a populist or reformist ideology.

From 1974 to 1982 the party suffered a rapid erosion of support in elections that were increasingly boycotted by the population as meaningless (see box above). For much of the period the party clung to its very survival by seeking a quota of seats in right-wing dominated Congresses that were condemned to irrelevance by the rapidly unfolding civil war. In order to win army support for the 1978

Ricardo Peralta Méndez on mild reformist platform. Probably comes third in elections in which 36.5 per cent of the registered electorate vote for the parties offered. Its representation in Congress is reduced to three.

1979: Rejects participation in the Democratic Front Against Repression (FDCR), a broad front of popular and democratic forces.

1980: Comes fourth in municipal elections in which 15 per cent of the electorate vote for the parties on offer.

1982: Forms United National Opposition (UNO) with the National Renovation Party (PNR) after abandoning idea of broad front with sections of the military. Alejandro Maldonado, ex-member of the MLN, leads the UNO in fraudulent presidential elections in which 35 per cent of the registered electorate vote. Party initially supports the Ríos Montt coup in March, although it later distances itself from the regime.

1984: In the Constituent Assembly elections of 1 July the party wins the highest percentage of the valid vote (15.6 per cent), and 20 of the 88 Congressional seats.

1985: In first round of presidential elections in November, Vinicio Cerezo wins 38.6 per cent of valid votes, 300,000 more than his nearest rival. The DCG also wins around three-quarters of the country's elections for mayors, and 51 of the 100 seats in Congress. In the second round in December, Cerezo wins 68 per cent of the vote from Jorge Carpio Nicolle of the National Union of the Centre (UCN).

1986: On 14 January Cerezo is sworn in as the first Christian Democrat President in Guatemala's history.

elections, the party again chose a military candidate, General Peralta Méndez, whose reputation was that of a 'moderate' or 'pro-development' officer. He was formerly head of the National Reconstruction Committee (CRN), which after the 1976 earthquake coordinated 'civic action' schemes, widely seen as a euphemism for the army's social control programme.[8]

The social-democrat parties like the FUR and the PSD called for a boycott of the 1978 elections and later joined the Democratic Front Against Repression (FDCR), which was a broad coalition of over 170 organisations including the main labour and peasant federations, students, slum-dwellers, and the ecumenical Justice and Peace Committee. Despite the repression that had already started against some Christian Democrat activists, the Christian Democrats not only refused to join the FDCR, but attacked it. As one social-democrat critic later described the Christian Democrats' decision: 'Faced with a revolution, the historical destiny of the Christian Democrat Party was to side with the dominant groups. This decision placed them squarely on the same plane as the forces of repression, and not on the side of democratic and popular forces.'[9]

When General Lucas García (1978-1982) turned his attention to the Christian Democrats as part of his general offensive against 'the centrist option', the result was the murder of at least 300 middle-ranking and provincial Christian Democrat leaders. Despite the worst period of repression in the party's history and the temporary closure of its headquarters in Guatemala City in 1981 after a shoot-out with Lucas' forces, Christian Democrat Congressmen spent most of the period 'calling for national dialogue and developing their parliamentary activity.'[10] Although 120 Christian Democrat members were killed in the twelve months before the March 1982 elections, the Christian Democrats once again refused to deny a military government a semblance of credibility and participated in an alliance with the PNR, a small 'moderate' party which had split off from the MLN. In the time-honoured tradition of outgoing military Presidents, Lucas García tried to impose his own choice on the Guatemalan electorate, but this time he was prevented by a military coup instigated by a group of young officers. This coup was in part motivated by the latest round of fraudulent elections.[11] According to one version of events, General Ríos Montt, the former Christian Democrat candidate for the 1974 elections, was teaching Sunday school in the church where he had previously been 'born again' when a group of officers contacted him and asked him to join them.

The Christian Democrats' initial reaction was to join the MLN in organising a rally in front of the National Palace in support of the coup. They hoped it would signify a rapid return to clean elections. Although Ríos Montt proved reluctant to keep his administration as transitional as the parties had hoped, and flirted with the idea of creating his own political base through a new Social Christian Party, the Christian Democrats maintained a position of tacit support until the later stages of his 18-month rule. They collaborated with government programmes, failed to condemn the bloody army massacres being carried out in the Guatemalan highlands (which further eroded the party's support amongst the Indian population), and went along with new legislation for the July 1984 Constituent Assembly elections despite an earlier insistence that Ríos Montt should put an end to Special Tribunals, which were newly-established military courts designed to put on trial suspected guerrillas.

The reasons for their cautious support probably lay in the links that existed between the Christian Democrat leadership and some of the younger officers supporting Ríos Montt, and the similarities between the latest coup and the revolt which some of the party had called for after the 1974 fraud.[12] When in August 1983 General Mejía Víctores stepped in to overthrow Ríos Montt in a coup that partly represented the return to power of a harder-line faction of the officers, it was no coincidence that the party was more vociferous in its complaints against the army.

Losing Links...

The party's failure to oppose the 1974 fraud and its unshakeable belief in the primacy of elections and parliamentary activity put a severe strain on its credibility. Not only had its electoral support been eroded but the fraud also accelerated the process by which it was losing its links with an organised social base. Important changes were taking place within the popular organisations. Trade unionists, church activists, students and both *ladino* and Indian *campesinos* were rapidly developing a consciousness, a programme and a level of organisation that went way beyond the orbit of Congress or the traditional political parties. After 1974 the Christian Democrats underwent major divisions: while left-wing sectors of the party and large parts of its social base left to join or ally themselves with the popular organisations, the bulk of the leadership — at best pragmatic, at worst opportunistic — looked towards the right.

The four years from 1973 to 1976 were key years for mass organisation in Guatemala. The most important umbrella organisation for this was CNUS (National Committee for Trade Union Unity), which was formed in March 1976, spearheaded by the CNT (National Workers Confederation). The CNT had been set up in 1968 along Christian Democrat lines and with its main support coming from the Christian Democrat-orientated FECETRAG and peasant leagues of the FCG. By the mid-1970s the CNT had emerged as the leading force in labour struggles. It was increasingly devoting itself to grassroots union issues and not to supporting Christian Democrat positions either nationally or internationally. In March 1978 the CNT and a sizeable segment of the FCG finally broke with CLAT, the continental Christian Democrat union organisation. CLAT had been established in 1961 with close links with Latin American Christian Democrat parties and the aim of promoting a third way between capitalism and communism.

What precipitated the break was CLAT's criticism of CNT's alliance with the more Marxist trade unions. The grassroots members of the CNT unions rejected CLAT's position as working against the unity of the working class. As one writer described the significance of the break: 'A labour movement that had begun with the Christian Democrats, and many of whose leaders had originally emerged from Catholic Action, in a crisis took a stand with larger union solidarity.'[13] While many CNT leaders and Christian Democrat activists close to the CNT came to identify closely with the political-military organisation FAR (Rebel Armed Forces), the Christian Democrats as a party were left with little influence or support in the labour movement. The Christian Democrat current within the Guatemalan trade union movement was not to resurface until CLAT was allowed to return to Guatemala soon after the Ríos Montt coup in 1982 and oversee the slow restructuring of FECETRAG and other Christian Democrat unions.[14]

A similar radicalisation of Indian and church groups of initially Christian Democrat sympathies took place within the peasant movement. Even before the 1974 elections some Indian and peasant communities had already lost faith in the Christian Democrat Party through their involvement with more radical peasant unions and Christian base communities. Some Catholic Action leaders participated in the 1974 Christian Democrat electoral campaign, but the fraud shattered the already fragile hopes of many *campesinos* that change could be brought about through elections or that the Christian Democrats could act as their voice.[15] In the same way that more progressive urban organisers left the party, the 1974 experience hastened the process by which the party's Indian and *campesino* constituency turned more towards popular organisations like the CUC (Committee for Peasant Unity).

By the late 1970s CUC had become the largest peasant organisation in the highlands and south coast of Guatemala, and worked closely with the EGP (Guerrilla Army of the Poor) in some areas. For many Guatemalan *campesinos* the experience was similar to that of Salvadorean peasants in the 1970s who originally supported the Salvadorean Christian Democrat Party, especially through their involvement in the peasant union FECCAS, but became progressively disillusioned over the party's participation in the fraudulent elections in the 1970s and doubted its chances of changing anything in El Salvador.[16]

...But Courting New Friends

As the base sought new solutions on the left, so the party leadership sought new options with the right. In fact the general path of the DCG's politics after 1974 can largely be explained by its leaders' desire to show an acceptable face to influential sectors within the triangle of forces which dominated Guatemalan politics — the military, the business community and, less importantly, the US colossus to the north. This new strategy did not amount in practice to the forging of cast-iron alliances with any of the three. Rather it lay in seeking at best points of coincidence with them, or at worst their acceptance of a possible Christian Democrat victory.

It was almost exclusively the party leadership which decided policies. The slow erosion of the party's grassroots support exacerbated the concentration of power at the top. There was little direct consultation with the rank-and-file, and the internal battles that took place (for example in the fight between Cerezo and de León Schlotter for the leadership of the party during the 1970s) were mostly waged within a narrow circle of leaders. One Guatemalan newspaper columnist recently described the party as fundamentally 'elitist':

> The DCG is a closed party, whose leadership is not affected by the opinion of its rank-and-file. Over time the names have changed but the style remains the same. In the 1960s it was de León, Barillas, Gelhert Matta, Gabriel Aguilera, and two or three more. In the seventies it was only de León, with Barillas, Cerezo and Cabrera, and in the eighties — when they finally came to power — those giving the orders are probably only Cerezo and Cabrera. The circle of leaders — far from expanding or becoming more democratic — has narrowed.[17]

Soon after the 1974 debacle, Danilo Barillas, the then DCG Secretary General, resigned from the party arguing that the DCG participation in Congress was 'a joke at the people's expense'. He later published a book entitled *Christian Democracy and its Position on the Army*, subtitled *A Call for an Historic Compromise*. The call was for reformist officers to launch a coup against the Laugerud government with support from civilian politicians like himself. Although the DCG had put forward military candidates in previous elections, Barillas' plea marked the beginning of a definite long-term Christian Democrat strategy to come to power by appealing to 'moderate' factions of the military who would be more willing, so the leadership hoped, to accept some minor reforms, some development in the rural areas, and a partnership with the DCG.

The policy of building coalitions was taken up again in 1977 by Vinicio Cerezo, by then the Secretary General of the party. In a remarkable but little-known pamphlet called *The Army: An Alternative*, Cerezo wrote of the need for the party to change its view of the Guatemalan army: it was no longer fundamentally anti-

---

The Army: An Alternative

'We must change our traditional vision of the army, in the sense that we must move on from viewing the army as an enemy of democratic parties and arrive at the position of possibly accepting them as an ally of these parties.

What we are suggesting here is that progressive politicians and military officials have a joint responsibility in the destiny of these countries and that both sectors must share the nation's decision-making.

In answer to the question of how are we going to achieve the above aims [of developing the country], the obvious response is that only two sectors could direct such a process: a progressive political party, with a wide popular base, discipline and an awareness of its historic task – like the Christian Democrat Party; and an organisation which has the right technical formation in the values of discipline, order and the exercise of power — like the Guatemalan Army.

We must tear down the barriers that impede communication between two of the national forces that can rely on organisation, discipline and progressive ideology. They are the Army and the Christian Democrat Party.

The present social, economic and political conditions suggest that there will be no positive solution unless the two sectors UNITE and make a gigantic and combined effort to reorganise and reorient the country.'

Source: Vinicio Cerezo, *The Army: An Alternative*, Guatemala, 1977.

---

democratic, but an instrument for social change; and only the DCG and the army together could develop the country (see box above). At the time of publication, the pamphlet represented a justification of the party's nomination of a military candidate for the 1978 elections, but it also painted an uncannily accurate picture of the cooperation that developed between the army and the DCG ten years later.

Neither Barillas' nor Cerezo's appeal proved successful. The bulk of the Guatemalan army remained power-greedy, corrupt, and more disposed towards the ultra-right-wing parties or parties of its own creation. However, some contacts were fostered between party leaders and a very limited number of officers, who probably even then recognised the points of coincidence between the Christian Democrats' developmentalism and their own 'social programmes', and the advantage of this approach as a more effective counter-insurgency measure than simply murdering leftist opposition.

Although such contacts were rarely made public, it was widely believed that some of the junior officers who supported Ríos Montt were DCG sympathisers, while Cerezo was said to enjoy good personal relations with such officers as Julio Caballeros (later to become his Chief of Police) and later Julio César Ruano (Mejía's Chief of Staff).[18]

However, for the right wing of the party, the search for the supposed reformism of some officers acted more as a smokescreen for political opportunism than as an expression of genuine ideological agreement. In the 1982 presidential elections, the right wing was pushing to join a staunchly far-right alliance which included the hand-picked successor of Lucas García, General Aníbal Guevara, as its candidate. Although Guevara was notorious for his military incompetence and corruption while Minister of Defence, de León detected certain 'social leanings' in him, which would allow more space for the party.[19]

Relations between the party and the US government grew warmer during President Carter's term of office. As in El Salvador and Nicaragua, Carter was always on the look-out for moderate options between the extreme right and revolutionary left. Cerezo's ability to project himself and the party as a centrist, non-violent and electorally-oriented alternative found some sympathy amongst US Democrats in Congress and the US liberal establishment. In this he was considerably helped by being the victim of at least three assassination attempts under Lucas (see box, pages 74-5), and by the presence in Washington of a team of lobbyists after 1980. They included his wife, Raquel de Blandón, a personal friend and successful businessman, Oscar Padilla (later to become Cerezo's Ambassador to the US), and later Francisco Villagrán Junior, working from the Guatemalan embassy.

The party's international credibility was also advanced by the presence of de León Schlotter, then honorary President of the World Christian Democrat Union and Honorary President of the DCG, at a seminal May 1980 meeting at the American Enterprise Institute in Washington. The meeting was funded by North American foundations and the immensely powerful source of international Christian Democrat ideology and money, the West German Konrad Adenauer Foundation. Its main purpose was to bring together Christian Democrat leaders and members of the US 'New Right' Santa Fé Committee to seek common ground between the military and Christian Democrats as a possible political formula for resolving the Central American crisis.[20] The most obvious product of such thinking was the 'legalised counter-insurgency' model applied in El Salvador. But different political circumstances in Guatemala meant that Cerezo was never promoted or financed by the Reagan administration as

---

Leaders and Patrons of the DCG

Vinicio Cerezo: President of Guatemala. A 44-year-old lawyer and graduate of USAC, and active student leader in the FESC. Became Secretary General of the party in 1976, and wrote *The Army: An Alternative* in 1977 arguing for a strategic alliance between the army and the DCG. He has survived at least three assassination attempts, which probably explains why he is a black belt in judo, travels with a small arsenal of weapons (justifying it on the grounds that 'democrats cannot afford to be naive') and subscribes to *Soldier of Fortune*. Before the 1985 elections, he represented the more progressive wing of the party in conflict with more conservative sectors around de León Schlotter, but has since moved to more 'pragmatic' positions.

Roberto Carpio Nicolle: Vice-President of Guatemala. A 56-year-old journalist, businessman and ex-professor at the Rafael Landívar University. Originally a member of the MLN, he has been a loyal DCG member for two decades. He was a founding partner of the newspaper *El Gráfico* together with his brother Jorge Carpio Nicolle, the paper's present owner and head of the UCN (Union of the National Centre). He also has economic interests in other news and graphic art businesses.

René de León Schlotter: The patriarch of the party, and one of its original founders. A lawyer, USAC professor, and specialist in agrarian law. Still represents the more right-wing faction. For many years was the most important Christian Democrat leader both inside and outside the country, and at present Honorary President of the party. Noted for his international contacts especially through the World Christian Democrat movement, which he once headed. At present Minister for Development, although considered to have been marginalised within the party.

Napoleón Duarte had been. Rather he was seen as an acceptable, but not necessarily favoured, anti-communist alternative to military rule. International support was far more forthcoming from the Konrad Adenauer Foundation, COPEI, and the Christian Democrat Party in El Salvador, both in terms of pro-Cerezo propaganda and financial support for his campaigns.

Reassuring the Right

Before the 1985 elections the DCG also made strenuous efforts to prepare the ground for acceptance by the final member of the ruling trio, the private sector. Although individual members of the agrarian

guarantee anti-reformist stance

Alfonso Cabrera: Has 23 years of active service in the party. In 1985 was named Secretary General of the party, and head of Congress in 1986. Made Minister for Special Affairs in January 1987. Considered to be second only to Cerezo in the party. Has close contacts with the Salvadorean Christian Democrat Party, for whom he served as an adviser in Duarte's 1984 electoral campaign. Regarded as a strong anticommunist. Known to be a presidential hopeful for 1990 elections.

Ricardo Gómez Gálvez: Assistant Secretary of the party, and replaced Cabrera as head of Congress in 1987. Ideologue and graduate of the Rafael Landívar University. Reputed to be close associate of de León.

Rodolfo Paiz Andrade: Minister of Finance. Personal friend of Cerezo, and not old party cadre. Joined the party in 1984 and said to have put sizeable amounts of money into party's campaign. Belongs to Paiz Ayala family, owners of Almacenes Paiz, a large chain of super-markets. Acts as key contact between the party and the private sector.

Juan José Rodil: Minister of the Interior. Lawyer and graduate of the Rafael Landívar University. Not a member of the party but close to it. Said to have advised Ríos Montt on dismantling the then secret police, the *judiciales*, and on the setting-up of the Special Tribunals. Director of legal department of Nestlé for Central America.

Fernando Andrade Díaz Durán: Although not at present a member of the party, was formerly an active member of the FESC and the DCG, and retains some contacts with the party. Foreign Minister for Mejía Víctores, and chief architect of Guatemala's independent foreign policy towards Central America. Married into the wealthy Falla coffee family, and said to be involved in business dealings with high military officials including investments in the Banco del Quetzal, whose other principal shareholder is General Lobos Zamora. At present Guatemalan representative at the United Nations and President of the Group of 77. Possible candidate for next presidential elections.

and industrial elites have enjoyed close family and ideological ties with parties like the MLN, PID, and CAN (Authentic Nationalist Central), it is CACIF which has tended to function as the most effective political pressure group for the private sector. Ever since its foundation in 1957, CACIF had been deeply mistrustful of the reformist strands within the DCG, arguing as in El Salvador that Christian Democrats were like water melons — 'green on the outside, but red on the inside.'

But in the run-up to the 1985 elections Cerezo and other Christian Democrat leaders removed, or at least neutralised, CACIF's suspicions by repeatedly reassuring them that the party's reformism lay firmly in its past. At a July 1984 meeting suitably held in the capital's sumptuous Camino Real Hotel, Cerezo joined the other presidential candidates in declaring that his party 'would not embark on banking or agrarian reforms, nor the nationalisation of companies or properties of the private sector,' as this would be 'disastrous for the economy and provoke capital flight'. On one occasion Cerezo even argued that 'there cannot be an agrarian reform in a democratic country, because that bankrupts or destabilises a country's economy'.[21]

But the party's overtures went beyond simply offering full guarantees to the privileges of the wealthy. Some common ground on economic policy was established between the neo-liberal technocrats of Cerezo's future economic team and a more modernising and dynamic group of businessmen who wielded the most influence within CACIF. Both were broadly agreed on the need to boost traditional agro-export production and to find new markets for non-traditional products, especially through the Caribbean Basin Initiative (CBI).

At the time of Ríos Montt and for some months after him, CACIF had been deeply fragmented. The two main organisations that represented landed capital, the older and more traditional Guatemalan Agriculturalists Association (AGA) and the newer and more modernising Chamber of Agriculture, nearly broke with the rest of CACIF when Ríos Montt lifted taxes on agro-exports but introduced VAT, which hit the commercial and industrial sectors. CACIF only began to re-unite towards the end of 1984 around its fierce and successful opposition to Mejía's attempts to push through a series of tax measures aimed at easing the severity of the economic crisis. Out of those battles CACIF emerged as a more cohesive force. The most influential group within it was a 'new generation' of younger business leaders, so called because many of them were the grandsons of some of oldest and richest Guatemalan families.

Alejandro Botrán, Pedro Lamport, Alvaro Castillo and Teddy Plocharsky were all third-generation members of families mentioned in Chapter 2. The first three were presidents of CACIF in 1985 and '86, while Plocharsky was head of UNAGRO (a merger of AGA and the Chamber of Agriculture in 1985). Traditional agro-exports like coffee and sugar remained the major source of wealth for this new generation, but many of them had the capacity and capital to switch to non-traditional agro-exports or industrial products. Although neither they nor CACIF formed a homogeneous group, these technically-trained and modernising businessmen tended to share the view that Guatemala's economic future lay in seeking new markets for traditional and especially non-traditional exports in the US and other western countries, rather than in the resurrection of the Central American Common Market through import substitution policies aimed at the region. They also favoured free-market policies and opposed the high level of state investment, which they said had only led to massive debt, a weak currency, and huge fiscal deficits through administrative and military corruption.[22] In this they concurred with the dominant neo-liberal Reaganite model for Central America, which aimed to serve local private enterprise and direct foreign investment by stimulating non-traditional exports through the Caribbean Basin Initiative.

After the recommendations of the 1984 Kissinger Report, USAID had stepped up its support for private enterprise in the region by setting up a number of new private sector organisations to promote the CBI. Although the Guatemalan version, the CAEM (Chamber of Business), failed to attract the support of most of the private sector (who at the time of its formation in 1982 were split and mostly suspicious of the CBI), other private development think tanks were established to seek export-oriented solutions to pull the economy out of its crisis. Most important of these were the USAID-funded FUNDESA, and FUNDAP, supported by the German Hans Seidel Foundation.

Christian Democrats had links into these initiatives. The head of CAEM, Guillermo Rodríguez, was said to be a key Cerezo backer within the business class, while Rodolfo Paiz Andrade, a member of the family owning the Paiz chain of supermarkets, was FUNDAP's ex-President and general coordinator of events. Paiz acted as a major funder of the DCG, and a central link between the party and the private sector (see box, pages 74-5). He was for a time posited as the Christian Democrat vice-presidential candidate, and later became Cerezo's first Minister of Finance. He and Cerezo also made trips to Miami to explain to North American investors what role Guatemala could play within the CBI.[23]

Cerezo also took advantage of the 'National Dialogue' which the Mejía government had set in motion in April 1985 to solve the CACIF-government impasse. He invited top personalities close to the private sector to participate in a future Christian Democrat government. This all helped to forge contacts, reduce CACIF's suspicions of the party and increase the common ground for the future. A key figure was technocrat and Christian Democrat sympathiser Lizardo Sosa, who enjoyed good personal connections with Pedro Lamport and Federico Linares — they had all studied together at the conservative Rafael Landívar University. This would considerably smoothe the way for negotiations over Cerezo's first economic package in March 1986 when Sosa would be Minister of the Economy, Linares head of the Central Bank and Lamport head of CACIF.

To be sure, the links between the party and CACIF were limited to a few businessmen, but all but the most reactionary members of the Guatemalan elites were reassured by the 'new responsibility' of the party. The rejection of reforms, the personal contacts between DCG members and the more modernising and influential sector within a reconstructed CACIF, and a broad agreement on the general direction of Guatemala's economic future all helped to strengthen the party's acceptance within the private sector. Unlike Napoleón Duarte, locked in a permanent state of war with the Salvadorean right, Cerezo would enjoy at least the tolerance, if not the support, of Central America's most powerful and privileged economic class.

By the time of the 1985 elections, the DCG was not a party of the poor. Although its party structures spread through most of Guatemala, since the early 1970s it had lost many of its links with organised *campesinos* and workers either through desertion or repression. Nor was the DCG a strongly ideological or reformist party. Rather, since 1974 its opportunistic leaders had gone in search of Guatemala's traditional power groups. Like the Salvadorean Christian Democrat Party, whose electoral victory through the National Opposition Union had been blocked by the army in 1972, the DCG had been vetoed by the Guatemalan military in 1974. Both parties had suffered internal splits, losing some of their base to the left, while their leadership had clung to electoral legality and moved to the right. Both were accepted by their respective armies as possible partners in a counter-insurgency strategy for the 1980s.

4.
Cerezo's Choice

'For convenience sake a civilian government is preferable, such as the one we have now; if anything goes wrong, only the Christian Democrats will get the blame. It's better to remain outside: the real power will not be lost.' Colonel D'Jalma Domínguez, former army spokesman.

For the Guatemalans queuing up at the polling stations, the 1985 presidential elections hardly represented the return of a long-lost freedom. Ever since the CIA-engineered coup in 1954 there had been plenty of elections — first in 1958, and then every four years from 1966 to 1982. But the ritual of the ballot box had never acted as a motor for social change — or, to use a phrase of Eduardo Galeano's, elections had been 'a joke on the people who have nothing and decide nothing'. *Inforpress* has accurately described them: 'Political parties functioned, candidates campaigned, and political platforms were debated, but the winners at best exercised formal power in the interests of those who had real political and economic control.'[1] There was little to suggest in the background to the 1985 elections that this new call to the urns would herald a significant departure from the past.

The Need for Elections

The elections were always intrinsically linked to the army's counter-insurgency strategy. Ever since Ríos Montt's March 1982 coup the return to civilian government had been seen as an integral part of the army's annual blueprints for fighting the revolutionary forces of the URNG. The so-called 'National Plan for Security and Development', which Ríos Montt himself claims to have dictated, was endorsed just one week after the coup. The main significance of the Plan lay in its decisive shift of emphasis from purely physical annihilation of the guerrillas towards ensuring permanent access to their popular support, and then enforcing mass involvement in the army's civilian patrols and development programmes. But at a national level it also stressed the importance of a return to constitutional rule. Points 12 and 14 of the Plan spoke explicitly of the need both to 'restructure the electoral system so that [...] there will be respect for political participation and avoidance of frustration among the people' and 'to reestablish constitutional rule in the country as a matter of urgency'.[2] The Mejía government also pledged its support for a two-stage electoral timetable of withdrawal. Both stages were firmly placed within the army's counter-insurgency plans for 1984 and 1985. 'Institutional Renewal '84' included a scheduling of elections for a Constituent Assembly on 1 July 1984, while 'Stability '85' called for presidential elections in 1985. Elections were clearly perceived to be more of a security issue than an expression of popular will.

For the army, there were numerous advantages to carefully stage-managing the election of a civilian President. Internationally, this would help to salvage the country's reputation as one of the worst (if not the worst) human rights violators in the western hemisphere, and act as a convenient smokescreen for continuing the fight against the URNG. Internally, the electoral game would go some way towards reconciling tensions with the tolerated political parties and reducing the legitimacy of the armed left. But there was also a more pressing need for the army's partial withdrawal from government. Throughout 1985 the Mejía regime was suffering intense political instability because of its failure to resolve the economic crisis. A fierce showdown with the private sector in April over tax increases and massive street protests in August and September against price rises nearly caused Mejía's downfall. Without the promise of the November elections, Mejía Víctores might not have lasted out the year.

The crisis convinced the majority of senior officers that a civilian regime would both take the heat off the army for its mismanagement of the economy and also possess greater moral authority to stop the economic decline. There was also the crucial question of aid: the appalling human rights record of the Mejía government had proved a real obstacle to securing dollars. A civilian President could secure substantial increases in economic and military aid, both as a way out of the economic morass and to help finance the war.

There were only two possible drawbacks. The first was whether a civilian government would attempt to question or control the army's counter-insurgency programme. Ever since Ríos Montt's National Plan, the army had been able to consolidate its political control over former conflict areas basically through the installation of its 'unholy trinity of control' consisting of civilian patrols, 'development poles' and the Inter-Institutional Coordination Committees (IICs). The 900,000 enforced members of the patrol system were the linchpin of the programme, but the 50 or so model villages in the six 'development poles' were equally important. The IICs were in effect a decentralised parallel government in the rural areas, by which the army could integrate the functions of various state agencies and ensure that all development projects and allocation of resources were subject to their final authority. The underlying aim was to win the hearts and minds of the Indian survivors by channelling money and resources into small-scale and low-cost social programmes. All three elements of the unholy trinity were written into the new Constitution being prepared by the Constituent Assembly. The whole system allowed the army to retain its control over the rural population, even under a future civilian government.

Moreover, defiant statements made by a number of regional commanders before the elections clearly showed that any civilian President would meet enormous obstacles in trying to dismantle such a deeply implanted system. 'The army expects the civilian government to respect the military plans against subversion,' was a typical warning from Colonel Edgar Hernández, commander of the Cobán military base, just three months before the elections. 'The army believes the civilian government will inherit a solid organisation — the proof of this is the IICs.'[3]

Most of the army's senior command were willing to accept a tactical withdrawal from open power, once the necessary measures had been passed to guarantee the consolidation of its counter-insurgency policy. In one sense the Guatemalan elections were repeating the US-inspired pattern set by the elections in Honduras (1981) and El Salvador (1984), whereby military or military-dominated governments were coaxed by the US into surrendering formal power to civilian governments (who often promised reforms), while the army remained firmly in control of security issues. But in the Guatemalan case control over security issues meant control over most of the country. As the North American magazine, *NACLA*, observed just before the elections:

> The army has saturated the Guatemalan countryside with barracks and bases, regular troops and paramilitary patrols, resettlement camps and model villages. It has created a complex fabric of new agencies, programs and bureaucratic structures, and begun to address new ways of organizing the rural economy [...] the army may be going back to the barracks, but in its definition the barracks cover most of Guatemala.[4]

The only other problem was the possibility that a new President would try to initiate trials of military personnel accused of atrocities.

But it soon became clear that none of the parties, including the DCG, was advocating prosecutions for past offences or seriously questioning the army's control over the rural areas. With the most moderate candidate offering solid guarantees both to the army and the private sector, the acceptability of a civilian President was put beyond doubt. The advantages of not putting up military candidates and overseeing a relatively free electoral process — in which no-one could doubt the purity of the event — far outweighed any particular preference that officers may have held.

The Best Hope

In the first round of elections on 3 November 1985, Vinicio Cerezo won a clear majority of 300,000 votes over his nearest rival, Jorge Carpio Nicolle of the Union of the National Centre (UCN). The official US government team of observers, headed by Richard Lugar, described the first round as 'free and fair'. On the face of it, the 1985 presidential elections did constitute an advance on the previous three contests. But the elections were free of fraud and military candidates because the army neither needed nor wanted to intervene too openly. Despite the plethora of parties, giving the impression of genuine political pluralism, only the small, exiled and previously heavily repressed Social Democrat Party (PSD) could plausibly be described as left of the Christian Democrats. The PSD had agreed to participate after Mejía himself had travelled to Costa Rica in January 1984 to persuade the party to take part in exchange for dropping the requirement for a minimum of 5,000 registered members. The *Financial Times* described the elections as a 'line-up of four extreme right parties and two right-wing parties, one centre-right with a token centre-left grouping, the Social Democrats, [...] providing little more than window dressing.'[5]

Nor was the human rights situation conducive to a free choice. An independent delegation sponsored by the Washington Office on Latin América stressed the general climate of political violence 'in which parties and voters were subject to various forms of intimidation', and the degree to which some of the population, especially Indian, voted through fear of the various penalties for not voting.[6] Travelling through various Indian departments six months after the elections confirmed the view that the major reason why many peasants had voted was their fear of a Q5 fine if they failed to vote — more than the daily income of at least 30 per cent of the Guatemalan population. In addition, a substantial proportion simply wanted their identity cards stamped as proof of having voted, so as not to run the considerable risk of being labelled a 'subversive' at army checkpoints.

In the run-off against Carpio Nicolle, Cerezo gained 68 per cent of the vote, giving him a wider margin of victory and a higher total vote than any Guatemalan President since Juan José Arévalo in 1944. The DCG also won a majority of 51 seats out of a possible 100 in the Congress, and 73 per cent of the country's mayors. Despite the high levels of abstentions in both the first and second rounds (31.5 per cent and 34.5 per cent respectively), the size of his majority and the large number of demonstrators present at Cerezo's victory rallies made it hard to deny that Cerezo had considerable, if conditional, support.

The high number of Christian Democrat mayors was solid evidence of the DCG's success in rebuilding its local level organisations after the Lucas García offensive. Cerezo also ran a much more efficient campaign, considerably aided by the DCG symbol of a white star in the pre-Christmas weeks and by Carpio's evident lack of intellectual precision and ineffectual championing of the UCN's 'nationalism' and 'centrism' as against the DCG's 'internationalism' and 'leftism'. The 'charm factor' also came into play, with most Guatemalans referring to Cerezo by his Christian name, 'Vinicio'. But the most convincing explanation for the Christian Democrat success lay in the DCG's reputation for being the party least involved in the corruption and repression of military governments. The fact that they had never actually assumed office offered the most appeal to the middle classes, who were tired of the army's corruption and mismanagement of the economy, and the best hope to the bulk of the population, who voted for the candidate most distanced from army savagery and apparently least unlikely to reject some sort of social reform. In short, the vote was seen not as a positive vote for Cerezo, but as a negative vote against the army.

The Acceptable Alternative

There was no possibility of a coup. As argued in Chapter 3, the DCG had carefully prepared the ground for their acceptance by the ruling trio. In some ways they were the most attractive party of convenience. For the Reagan administration, the priority was first that the elections should take place and secondly that they should be clean. Although the State Department would probably have favoured a more anti-Sandinista candidate like Jorge Serrano Elías of the PDCN (Democratic Party of National Cooperation), any cleanly elected civilian President was useful both as a way of increasing US leverage over Guatemalan politics and as a means to step up US propaganda against the only 'undemocratic' country in the region — Nicaragua. After all, although Cerezo would pursue a peaceful solution to the region's problems, the Salvadorean example proved that Christian Democrats could be useful partners in counter-insurgency plans. Furthermore, the DCG represented a much better option than the antiquated ultra-right parties like the MLN, PID or CAN. The international climate favoured new 'moderate' faces, who could not be so easily associated with a semi-fascist ideology or past acts of repression.

Although Carpio Nicolle or Serrano Elías may have been the preferred choice of the private sector, the DCG offered the best prospect of more economic aid and investment because of its international credibility and contacts. As already argued, both the links between the party and business representatives and the reassurances about the need to avoid reforms convinced all but the most reactionary CACIF members that their privileges would not be under attack. In fact CACIF was said to have given at least Q40,000 (US$16,000) to the Christian Democrat campaign (as it did to virtually all the candidates).[7]

The army too was reassured by the 'new responsibility' of the DCG. The party certainly represented a better option than the far-right parties. Many regional commanders had become painfully aware of the limitations of their Manichean East-West schema for interpreting the causes of the civil war, and by now recognised the advantages of social programmes to undercut support for the URNG. Moreover, according to some reports, most of the senior command, including some of the old guard, swung their support behind Cerezo after he had humiliated Carpio Nicolle in a televised debate. A week before the elections, Cerezo even revealed to two US journalists a confidential memorandum from military intelligence predicting a victory for the DCG 'due to the links they had forged with the army, as well as with the US'.[8]

There was also frequent speculation about a possible pact between the military and the DCG. The precedent always cited was the deal struck between the army and the last civilian President in Guatemala, Julio César Méndez Montenegro of the Revolutionary Party (PR). Méndez Montenegro was only allowed to assume the office he had won in the 1966 elections after he had signed an agreement with the army. As a result of a nine-point pact, Méndez relinquished all but nominal power, and gave the army complete independence to wage its brutal war against the Rebel Armed Forces (FAR) in the east of the country. Cerezo claimed that he would never make such a compromise. According to an article in the *New York Review of Books*, 'before the elections Cerezo promised that he would never submit to such humiliation, that he would rather resign and provoke a coup to show up the army's hollow pledges — and cause a popular uprising — than stay in office as the military's stooge."[9]

Despite Cerezo's assurances, events over the first twelve months of his government convinced many Guatemalans that he may have arranged some sort of spoken deal that tied his hands, even though it had never emerged publicly. How else was it possible to explain his failure to change anything, precisely at the time he enjoyed most popular support?

1986 — A Year of Disappointment

The fact that the army had largely dictated the rationale for the elections clearly established the limits on Cerezo's room for manoeuvre. He himself estimated that he would only have 30 per cent of the power when he took office, and 70 per cent when he left. But there was just a hope that he would interpret his massive majority as a plebiscite for change. After all, his party enjoyed widespread internal and international support, and neither the US government, the army nor the private sector was likely to promote a coup in the first few months of his government.

Instead Cerezo opted for caution and staying in government. At his inaugural speech he pleaded for time and understanding to help him consolidate civilian power after 30 years of disastrous military rule. But just six months after his victory, most observers were already arguing that he had 'missed the boat', or that he had confused patience with convenience. Cerezo's rhetoric spoke of reaching consensus — known locally as *concertación* — between all sectors of the Guatemalan population, including the poor. But Cerezo clearly made it his priority to reach consensus with the business community and with the faction of the army which was prepared to allow him to stay in office. His political strategy was based on not confronting the military but working with them, while his blueprint for the economy was to halt the decline by seeking both the confidence of the private sector (so that they would invest) and a gold rush of new foreign aid. The final ingredient was a foreign policy of 'active neutrality' in the region, skilfully designed to secure new friends and money. As *Le Monde Diplomatique* observed, 'everything happens as if Cerezo had only one idea in his head: to avoid a coup.'[10] The formula worked well for his own political survival but not for the 63 per cent of the Guatemalan population struggling to survive below the official poverty line.

On the surface Guatemala appeared less militarised. There were fewer soldiers on the streets, fewer military checks in the rural areas, and no army officials in government except the Minister of Defence.

General Jaime Hernández, Colonel Roberto Mata, Vinicio Cerezo, and
General Héctor Gramajo, Guatemala City, Army Day 1986

But behind the scenes Cerezo was successfully courting a loose
grouping of 'moderate' officers who together formed the most
influential sector within the army's senior command. They included a
significant number of colonels who had direct experience of the army's
'development' programmes, like Roberto Mata Gálvez, former head
of the Santa Cruz del Quiché base, and now presidential chief of staff;
Colonel Enrique Paiz Bolaños, ex-head of S-5 (the army's Civic
Affairs unit), and now vice-presidential chief of staff; and Colonel
Eduardo Wohlers, famous for his love of kibbutzim-style solutions for
the Guatemalan countryside, and at present head of S-5. These
officers were widely rumoured to centre on the then army chief of staff
and strong man, General Héctor Gramajo. They enjoyed the support
of middle-ranking officials and had the reputation of being less corrupt
and more professional as soldiers. They were also ardent advocates of
the need for the army to continue, and maintain control over, the
various branches of its counter-insurgency programme.

These officers were prepared to see Cerezo stay in office, against the
desires of more recalcitrant (and more corrupt) officers who tended to
group around the ex-chief of staff under Mejía, General Lobos
Zamora. Lobos Zamora was accused by human rights groups of being
the intellectual author of some of the worst repression perpetrated by
previous regimes. He was tipped to be the Minister of Defence in the
new government, but Cerezo reportedly managed to persuade the
military that Lobos' appointment would look too much like a
continuation of the past. Although Lobos was not retired, he was at

least shipped off to Panama as ambassador, reputedly suitably placed to further his interest in the narcotics trade and, in the words of Cerezo, 'far enough away from Guatemala City not to plot against the government'.[11]

The rest of the command structure remained intact. General Jaime Hernández was made Minister of Defence, and, although a compromise choice, he was hardly a liberal: in 1980-1 he had been in command of special operations in Playa Grande in the north of Quiché — an area of strong guerrilla activity and army repression at the time. When head of the elite Guard of Honour from 1982-5, he was the commanding officer of a G-2 (Military Intelligence) captain named Armando Villegas, who was said to have been closely involved in the horrendous killing of Beatriz Barrios on 11 December 1985. Barrios was a school teacher who was leaving for Canada on the Canadian government's refugee programme when the taxi taking her to the airport was intercepted. According to an article in the US magazine, *New Republic*:

> The next morning Villegas was seen by a group of his colleagues by the side of a highway south of the capital standing over Barrios's naked and mutilated body. A note in Villegas' handwriting had been placed on the corpse saying, 'More to come'. After the killing, Captain Villegas was made a director of Cerezo's Presidential Guard.[12]

Even those officers more willing to go along with the 'democratic experiment' were bound to have had heavy involvement in past acts of repression. The likelihood of such acts continuing remained high as many officers notorious for past repression were still on active service. Moreover, although the Guatemalan army perceived themselves as victors in a 30-year war against international communism, the war was still going on and so required constant vigilance. They were clearly unwilling to surrender any of the security domain to civilians. Nowhere was this more evident than in the tension over who would wield control over the National Police.

On 29 June 1986 General Gramajo broke the army's ominous silence and made the first public criticism of the new government. In an interview published in the Sunday section of *Prensa Libre*, he made a thinly-veiled attack on the Minister of the Interior, Juan Rodíl. Rodíl had for some time been trying to reorganise and expand the police force with financial and technical help from Spain, West Germany and Venezuela. More importantly, he was making a serious attempt to place the police under civilian control, when under previous military governments the police simply took their orders from the army.

Gramajo complained openly that in the 'transition to democracy' the army had been scorned and unappreciated for its 'experience and familiarity in the area of protection'. On 14 July, the retired army officer and lawyer, Rubén Suchini Paiz, was summarily replaced as Head of Police by Colonel Julio Caballeros, an officer formerly linked to G-2 and known to be close to Gramajo and Cerezo. Although the formal role of the police is to be a tool for fighting common crime, Caballeros was quick to emphasise that they were 'in the front line of combat against subversion'. Later, the civilians in two other key security-related posts — heads of the Treasury Police and Immigration Office — were replaced with a senior army and navy officer. The message was clear: all security and counter-insurgency matters would remain under army control. The Christian Democrat government seemed unable or unwilling to question it.

Low-Intensity Democracy

Cerezo's apologists claimed that his working with the 'democratic' factions of the army — and apparently spending long hours at the Centre for Military Studies and on the presidential farm at Santo Tomás lecturing middle-ranking officers on the merits of democracy — was the only realistic way of slowly consolidating the transfer to civilian power. But the strategy of non-confrontation had its price. First, there was little indication that any transfer of power actually occurred, while no progress was made in investigating past human rights violations or preventing new atrocities. One catechist explained the change as 'Cerezo having a different face, but the army having the same teeth and the same claws'.

The crudeness of the image was justified by the sustained practice of forced disappearances, political executions and even occasional large-scale killings which continued behind the veneer of normality. There was to be no sharp break with the past. According to a letter signed by twelve pastoral workers from a parish in Izabal, and endorsed by the local bishop, in June seven refugees were 'disappeared' and an unspecified number of women and children massacred by soldiers. Although the letter made a strong plea to the Cerezo government to investigate the cases, no official committee was ever set up. Pedro Có [name changed] was a catechist and leader of a group of displaced Indians from Quiché hiding out in Guatemala City. At considerable personal risk Pedro had given details to the October 1984 British Parliamentary Human Rights Group of killings carried out by army-sponsored 'hit squads', who travelled down from highland villages to Guatemala City in order to pursue and pick off their victims. Pedro was 'disappeared' in May 1986, and his family warned not to report the case or they would suffer the same fate.

On 26 June a researcher for Americas Watch, Beatriz Manz, happened to be sitting in a café in Guatemala City's busy Zone 1 when she saw two men dressed in civilian clothes approach a young man and calmly fire five bullets into him. The two assassins did not rob the man, but quickly left the scene. The researcher only discovered by going to the hospital that the victim was a 29-year-old architectural student — the police did not give any details to the press. In fact, when they arrived at the scene of the crime, they made no attempt to talk to witnesses or seriously pursue the murderers. When Manz later wrote a feature for the *New York Times* based on the murder, Elliott Abrams, Reagan's Assistant Secretary of State and the contras' most energetic partisan, wrote a letter to the *Times* criticising Manz for her lack of objectivity, as 'the murder was reported in the Guatemalan press (*La Prensa*, June 27)'. Abrams' obsession with overthrowing the Sandinistas may have clouded his usually sharp mind. *La Prensa* is a Nicaraguan and not a Guatemalan newspaper, and the only reference to the murder was a short funeral notice for the victim in *Prensa Libre*.[13]

The last two cases are important because they suggest that human rights assessments based on the local press — such as the State Department's reports — underestimate the true extent of what happened during the first twelve months of Cerezo's term. Accurate monitoring was seriously hampered throughout 1986 by the absence of a professional and independent human rights office. Guatemala remained the only country in Central America where conditions did not permit the installation of such an office, although towards the end of the year Archbishop Penados did pledge to change this and start up an office some time in 1987, modelled on *Tutela Legal* in El Salvador. For those dispassionate enough to play the numbers game, the most quoted figures were: 126 politically-related disappearances and 463 extra-judicial assassinations in 1986 (according to the Mexico-based Guatemalan Commission for Human Rights, CDHG); 128 disappearances up to 15 November (the Mutual Support Group, GAM); or at least 224 killings and 110 disappearances in the first ten months of 1986 (*Inforpress*, using press figures).

The figures were undoubtedly lower than in previous years, but they hardly justified the absurdly extravagant claims of the government and the US embassy that 'patterns of abuse had stopped completely'.[14] Claiming substantive improvements on the basis of quantitative reductions and not qualitative change was bound to be unconvincing to most serious observers, especially when any variation was to be

The *New Republic* Affair

On 30 June 1986 the liberal rightist North American magazine, the *New Republic*, published an article entitled 'The Bureaucracy of Death', by US journalist Allan Nairn and the Americas Watch representative in Guatemala, Jean-Marie Simon. The article contained detailed information about the inner workings of G-2 and its responsibility for numerous cases of disappearances, torture and assassinations. The authors described G-2 as the 'non-elected government of Guatemala that Cerezo must find a way to control' which was 'more comfortably entrenched than at any time since the mid-1960s'. What was most remarkable about the article was that Nairn and Simon dared to name various G-2 officials allegedly responsible for the crimes, thereby transgressing the norms usually considered safe for practising journalists.

For example, they quoted military sources as saying that the then chief of the homicide division of the DIT, Jaime Martínez Jiménez, carried out the notorious killings of two GAM leaders in March and April 1985, while operating under the orders of a G-2 commander named Colonel Carlos Dorantes Marroquín. On 30 March, Héctor Gómez, a baker from Amatitlán, had been kidnapped after a GAM meeting. The following morning his body was dumped on a side road reportedly with his tongue cut out and his skin apparently burnt with a blow torch. Three days after Gómez's funeral, a second GAM leader, Rosario Godoy, her brother and two-year-old son were found dead in a ravine after what looked like a faked traffic accident. Rosario had promised at the funeral that Héctor's death would not be in vain. Rosario's body showed signs of having been sexually molested, while mourners at the wake noticed that her baby's fingernails were missing.

The article also contained information on the death of two of the country's leading social democrat politicians, Alberto Fuentes Mohr and Manuel Colom Argueta, who were killed within two months of each other in 1979. Their brutal murders were widely considered at the time to be one of the main catalysts of the escalating civil war. According to the journalists, 'the plans to kill the two politicians were relayed by General David Cancinos, who was then Minister of Defense and overseen by Colonel Héctor Montalván, who was presidential chief of staff [...] Montalván's chief aide at the time was an officer named Edgar Godoy Gaitán. Earlier this year, the army appointed Colonel Godoy to be the commander of the G-2.'

The sources for their information ranged from Cerezo himself to high-ranking officials under previous governments. Colonel D'Jalma Domínguez was one of the officers who talked to them: 'If under the concept [of being in a war], it means that the government has an apparatus dedicated to finding and eliminating people of the left, to me that is perfectly normal.' When news about the article finally surfaced⬧

in Guatemala City, Domínguez was quick to contend that the article was a distortion of what he had said, perhaps due to Nairn's 'lack of intelligence or Spanish', and threatened to sue the journalists for libel. Other officers like General Benedicto Lucas, ex-army chief of staff and brother to ex-President Lucas García, did not retract or deny any of their statements. Lucas had admitted that, 'if the G-2 wants to kill you, they will kill you. They send out one of their trucks with a hit squad — and that's it.'

Army spokesmen came out with a profusion of defensive statements aimed at discrediting the article. These ranged from explaining that it was normal for any army to have an intelligence branch to implying that the authors were allies of the URNG. Cerezo for his part declared that such acts were a thing of the past and denied that officers named in the article were occupying high military positions. But a few days earlier he had responded 'to a recent Americas Watch report by labelling the organisation 'liberal left — that's to say, extremist' and accusing it of using information that came from the guerrillas — a tactic inherited from his predecessors of attacking their critics and not addressing the subject of their criticisms.

Most Guatemalans were left wondering what all the fuss was about. They were faced with the odd sensation of hearing a series of denials, but not really knowing what is was that was being denied. Although the Guatemalan newspapers were given translations of the article, none dared to publish its substance. In addition, Guatemala has three press associations, whose supposed duty is to defend freedom of expression in the country, but they all ignored the incident. Practically the only information available to the general public was gleaned from a brief TV interview with Nairn after he had emerged from a meeting with Cerezo. With remarkable coolness Nairn told the cameras that the present chief of staff and Minister of Defence, Gramajo and Hernández, along with Generals Mejía Víctores, Lobos Zamora and Colonel Nuila Hub, had all participated in one way or another in operations like those described in the article. Much to the disbelief of many Guatemalans watching, Nairn added — not without a certain amount of irony — that he was not worried about his own safety, because 'President Cerezo had given him his personal guarantee of protection'. The two journalists were watched by security men before they left the country.

In a TV interview around the same time, Martínez Piedra, the US Ambassador to Guatemala, compared the respective situations in Guatemala and Nicaragua, and argued that 'here in Guatemala, you have freedom of expression'. He would have done well to read a *Newsweek* report of 28 July on the *New Republic* affair: 'Local journalists were unanimous: to cover the largest story in modern Guatemalan history, they risked being killed.'

explained more by the weakness of the left than by any civilian control over the security forces. The issue was whether the structure of repression remained intact, and consequently whether the 'new democracy' was still based on terror. A *New York Times* journalist wrote in 1983:

> Once war begins, the body count becomes a mere technical indicator of the ebb and flow of the Government campaign to kill suspected guerrilla sympathisers. They may kill them now or they may kill them later but they will kill them some time. Claiming human rights progress during a lull [...] is like detecting a change in a meat-packer's attitude because the slaughterhouse shuts down for a vacation.[15]

No-one blamed either Cerezo or his government ministers for ordering the killings or disappearances. But Cerezo's only significant action was to dismantle a group of largely expendable civilians working for the Department of Technical Investigations (the DIT). At the beginning of February 1986 the DIT was raided and subsequently disbanded. Only one of its former 600 agents was charged (with murdering one of his fellow officers), while the majority were rehired in other law-enforcement agencies, some of them into the newly-created Department of Criminal Investigations, which occupied the same building as the DIT. The move against the DIT was clearly designed as a showpiece exercise, similar to the one carried out by Ríos Montt in 1982, when the old judicial police was disbanded and renamed the DIT. It was politically possible because it did not touch G-2, the military intelligence unit, which remained at the core of the army's security operations, and one of the main obstacles to civilian control over the military (see box, pages 90-1).

The general climate of fear was maintained by Cerezo's refusal to cancel Decree No. 8-86, dubbed the 'army insurance policy'. Just before surrendering office the Mejía government had conferred upon itself an amnesty for all political crimes since the Ríos Montt coup. The Argentine military government had decreed itself a similar pardon just two weeks before the October 1983 elections, but one of the first and boldest acts of the Alfonsín government was to repeal the law. Cerezo however, remained true to his promise to draw a line under the past, and made no attempt to overturn the decree or to prosecute a single army officer. The Christian Democrat majority in Congress also failed to support a move by opposition parties to repeal both Decree 8-86 and another last-minute Mejía decree giving the army the right in perpetuity to import their luxury goods duty-free.

In November Cerezo even attempted to veto a law to set up an ombudsman or procurator empowered by the Constitution to investigate human rights abuses. Only incompetence and his vice-President's failure to act quickly enough stopped him from exercising his presidential right of veto, and the law was passed. It was clear that the Christian Democrat leadership was stepping on any initiative that might embarrass its cosy relationship with the military. Furthermore, there was considerable doubt whether much incriminating evidence would turn up, even if the army ever allowed an investigation to go ahead. Many Guatemalans would be too fearful of reprisals to give evidence, while some army officials claimed that there was no evidence to find. 'In Argentina there are witnesses, there are books, there are films, there is proof,' said one colonel; 'here in Guatemala there is none of that. Here there are no survivors.'[16]

Cerezo's 'hands-off' policy towards the army was bound to set him on a collision course with the Mutual Support Group for the Relatives of the Disappeared (the GAM). The GAM had been started in June 1984 by a small group of remarkably resilient and courageous women, some of whom had met for the first time in mortuaries while looking for their disappeared relatives. The barbarous killings of two of their leaders in March 1985 (see box, pages 90-1) had not prevented at least 1,000, mostly women, members from joining the group and stridently demanding serious investigations into at least some of the country's 38,000 disappeared (according to Americas Watch, this is equivalent to 42 per cent of the *desaparecidos* in all of Latin America). The GAM's efforts were given wide international support, which included 56 British MPs — among them Neil Kinnock and David Steel — who nominated the GAM for the 1986 Nobel Peace Prize.

Most GAM members suspected that their disappeared were dead. Nevertheless, they wanted to bring to justice those responsible for the disappearances and make Cerezo stick to his initial promise to set up an independent commission. In June Cerezo abruptly cancelled the plan. By the end of the year he had successfully stalled on a second promise to set up the commission, condoned the violent break-up of GAM demonstrations, and tried to buy off sectors of the GAM by offering them money to drop their demands. There was virtually no progress on investigating the 1,400-odd writs of habeas corpus filed by the GAM. Furthermore, on one occasion when some GAM members broke down in tears during a meeting with Cerezo, he momentarily dropped his customary charm, accused them of being 'masochistic' and told them 'not to poke around in the past'.[17] The persistence with which the GAM pursued their demands led to predictable claims that the group was manipulated by the guerrillas. 'There is absolutely no question of manipulation,' Nineth de García, the GAM's main leader, was forced to respond. 'We must know what has happened to the remains of our loved ones — it is a basic human need.'[18]

Maintaining the Fear

The army's control over vast swathes of the countryside remained non-negotiable. The increased, though still sporadic, presence of the URNG in eight of Guatemala's 21 departments only strengthened the army's refusal to surrender control over what it regarded as areas of legitimate security concern. This inevitably meant that soldiers and civilian patrols continued to rule by fear in many of the highland departments. Cerezo failed to make good his campaign promise to let the people decide the fate of the 900,000-member civilian patrols, described by the British Liberal peer, Lord Avebury, as the 'only example in recorded history when an army of occupation has been forged out of a native population'.[19] Although in some villages the patrols were disbanded, in remote or conflict areas the patrols stayed mandatory and under tight army control.[20]

Guatemala's spectacularly beautiful highland landscape remained scarred by the archipelago of resettlement areas, temporary camps, and sterile, jerry-built 'model villages'. Far from questioning the army's schemes, the new government helped them to consolidate the 'development' arm of their counter-insurgency plan. Just one month after being sworn in as President, Cerezo confirmed his approval of the model villages by inaugurating the Chisec 'development pole' in Alta Verapaz, which had already been inaugurated by the army before the elections. The new Minister of Development and Christian Democrat patriarch, René de León Schlotter, also cut the ribbon to inaugurate new public works at Bichivalá in the Ixil Triangle Development Pole. In many ways, their actions represented the confirmation of the ideological overlap between the army's brand of development and Christian Democrat ideology, and the successful culmination of the DCG's policy of courting more 'development-minded' officers like Ríos Montt and Peralta Méndez in the 1970s. Cerezo even claimed in a newspaper interview that the development poles had been part of the DCG programme since the 1960s, but added that the problem was who controlled them.[21]

Just after his appointment de León had also endorsed the army's version of development as a component of fighting the URNG. He stated categorically that the main purpose of his new Ministry was 'to combat subversion ideologically, in much the same way as the army has been doing through the Inter-Institutional Coordination System (IICs).'[22] The IICs were in fact formally replaced by Councils of

Development, and their military leaders replaced by 22 civilian governors, but during the year there was considerable confusion and political infighting as to who would ultimately administer the development poles: the Ministry of Development as originally intended, the Councils of Development (technically under the control of the Vice-President), or the army's National Reconstruction Committee (CRN — under General Fuentes Corado)? At the same time, the army was said to have trained 1,500 'social promoters' to work in the rural areas and administer their programmes, while the Ministry of Development was training 500 similar promoters to do similar work, possibly to act as organised support for the DCG. There was less doubt over who still actually controlled the various model villages, as evidenced by the ubiquitous military presence and the need for military permits to gain access to some of them.[23] The vast majority of the 40,000 recognised Guatemalan refugees — out of an unofficial total of around 150,000 — who had fled from the army terror to Mexico remained unconvinced by the prospect of civilian control over their former homes. The UNHCR estimated that only 343 trickled back across the border from January to October 1986.

The return to constitutional rule undoubtedly helped to create more room for a spate of mostly spontaneous protest demonstrations, and more freedom for unions to restart cautious and usually urban-based organisation. In part, the new political space flowed from the Christian Democrat Party's own need to restructure an organised social base. With the help of CLAT, the Konrad Adenauer Foundation, and Italian and Venezuelan Christian Democrat labour groups, major efforts and money were channelled into the reorganisation of a small social-Christian federation named CGTG (General Coordination of Guatemalan Workers), formally set up in March 1986. Although the CGTG eschewed public links with the Christian Democrat government and criticised Cerezo's economic package, it was frequently accused of being *oficialista*, or, more specifically, a personal vehicle for de León through his access to international Christian Democrat money and personal links with the CGTG's General Secretary, Julio Celso de León.

The two other larger union groupings, the CUSG, which receives money from the American Institute for Free Labor Development (AIFLD), and the independent and more radical UNSITRAGUA, took advantage of the new climate to step up their activities and profile. But it was a slow and cautious process, especially for UNSITRAGUA, which had grown out of the successful year-long occupation of the Coca-Cola factory in 1984-5 and grouped together around 25 of the more militant unions including the Coca-Cola workers, the glass-workers union in CAVISA, and the employees of USAC. UNSITRAGUA members were especially mindful of the 1980 union decapitation when security forces organised the mass disappearance of 44 leaders of two labour federations, Guatemala's equivalent of the British Trades Union Congress (TUC). Despite the new space, there were enormous economic, political and security obstacles to union organisation. Many workers understandably feared union involvement would jeopardise their tenuous hold on employment, since 50 per cent of the workforce was unemployed according to official figures. Secondly, the Christian Democrat government resisted union pressure to implement minimum wage legislation and also failed to push through urgently needed reforms of labour legislation — in fact, the Ministry of Employment was frequently accused of deliberately delaying unions' legal registration which could have strengthened their legal and financial bargaining positions with employers.

Furthermore, Cerezo's brash boast that 'under the new regime no politician, trade union or student leader had been repressed' was undermined by the widely-publicised cases of Justo Rufino Reyes (an official of the Municipal Workers Union, stabbed to death on 23 July 1986) and Edilio Viera Guzmán (Secretary General of the Street Vendors Union, who disappeared on 23 October 1986). In general, according to the 1987 British Parliamentary Human Rights Group (PHRG)/Americas Watch report, '[unions'] rank-and-file and potential activists simply do not believe it is safe in Guatemala to engage in open trade union activity.'[24] One young trade union leader from a US-owned manufacturing plant was deeply pessimistic about the future: 'We've seen this cycle before. Méndez Montenegro allowed the people a few liberties and Arana smashed them. Kjell allowed a few things and Lucas García smashed them. Now Vinicio will allow a few things and ... They allow the leaders to stick their heads up so they'll know whose to cut off when the time comes.'[25]

The Right to Buy

The inherent contradiction between allowing some degree of popular organisation and at the same time offering full guarantees to the private sector was highlighted by the sudden appearance of tens of thousands of mostly southern-based *campesinos* publicly organising and demanding land. By the beginning of 1987 there were an estimated 200,000 peasants organised into ten different groups, some of whom were already carrying out tentative land invasions in different parts of the country.

Father Andrés Girón, during a rally on 12 July 1986 at Nueva Concepción, Escuintla

By far the largest peasant group paid their Q1 or Q2 a month to become members of the National Peasant Association for Land (ANC), under the leadership of the messianic Father Andrés Girón. On 2 May a march organised by Girón arrived at Guatemala City to demand land for his peasants, many of whom had lost their jobs after the collapse of cotton production. With the march reportedly cleared with the army and with the buses laid on by the government to take them back to the south coast, 16,000 peasants walked up to 150 kilometres to Guatemala City, some carrying banners announcing that they had voted for Cerezo and not for the army or CACIF. Cerezo promised them a response within a month.

Two months later, on 12 July, around 5,000 gathered in Girón's home town of Nueva Concepción in Escuintla to hear the self-styled 'people's advocate' and Guatemala's first lady, Raquel de Blandón, as well as René de León Schlotter and the Minister of Agriculture, Rodolfo Estrada, make vague promises of land for the future. Finally, in the first week of December, 300 peasant families from Girón's movement were settled on a 1,500-acre run-down coffee plantation near Yepocapa in the foothills of the Fuego volcano in Chimaltenango. It was the first successful attempt to find land for the 50,000 peasants Girón claimed belonged to his movement. As the 300 families represented a tiny fraction of the country's 420,000 landless families, Girón had clearly lit the fuse to Guatemala's biggest political powder keg.

The precise nature of Girón's demands and ideology were sometimes hard to pin down. Describing himself as 'a guerrilla of Jesus' and his movement as embracing 'an ideology of hunger', Girón veered from demanding a nationwide agrarian reform and the immediate expropriation of 23 former *fincas* of García Granados to asking the government to facilitate private land purchases for his peasants; from lambasting UNAGRO as the 'number one robber in the country' to publicly blessing them; and from advocating land seizures to just as quickly asserting the peaceful nature of his movement. Critics accused him of wheeling and dealing with Cerezo or the DCG, and his movement of acting as a potential political base — allegations which he stoutly denied. But despite Girón's maverick qualities, most observers agreed that for the moment at least he was not calling for an expropriatory or confiscatory land reform. Rather, he was demanding the right for peasants to buy, at concessionary terms, underused private land mortgaged to state or private banks, which peasants could then farm collectively. To this end he sought financial support both from the government and from humanitarian or aid agencies in the US and Europe.

Girón's immediate demands loosely squared with long-held Christian Democrat ideology and USAID solutions to Guatemala's crushing land problem. In the 1970s de León Schlotter had written in a book called *A Path for Guatemala* that the best solution would be a better inventory of state-owned land and the stricter application of an idle-land tax, which would open the way for the state to claim and then distribute the land. In early 1986 the new Ministry of Agriculture also suggested a tax on idle land, but limited the rest of its proposals to simplifying land titling procedures.[26] USAID for its part had argued in a notorious 1982 study entitled *Land and Labour in Guatemala* that the way forward lay in the combination of an active land market, further colonisation schemes and joint worker-owner agricultural business schemes. Their most controversial suggestion was for a land bank to purchase farms at market prices and sell them at reduced prices to landless peasants. At the time the book had been labelled 'subversive' by big landowners who viewed any transfer of land to new owners via the state as tantamount to an agrarian reform. The then Agriculture Minister, Leopoldo Sandoval, had been forced to resign after supporting some of USAID's suggestions.

In August 1986 Cerezo finally announced the new government's response to the land question. He categorically rejected an expropriatory agrarian reform, which he dismissed as Marxist, confrontational, ruled out by the reality of contemporary politics and in any case discredited by the disastrous experience of USAID's programme in El Salvador. In its place he proposed a cautiously-named programme of 'Integrated Rural Development'. Although the programme was labelled 'one of the most important changes in the structure of land tenure and use in the last 40 years', it deliberately spoke only vaguely of 'land for peasants, technical assistance and product marketing.' It was left to the Minister of Agriculture, Rodolfo Estrada, to announce that up to 200 private estates had been offered for sale to the state in different parts of the country, which would help absorb the *campesinos'* demand for land. Although the exact physical, financial and legal status of these *fincas* was left unclear — some of them were available on the free land market, others were held by state banks or mortgaged to Guatemalan and foreign banks — the basic idea was that the government or the bureaucracy-riddled INTA (the National Institute of Agrarian Transformation) would act as intermediaries to help the peasants buy the *fincas* on concessionary terms. By early 1987 only four *fincas* had been publicly identified — the above-mentioned coffee farm in Chimaltenango, two banana estates on the south coast and one *finca* in San Marcos.

It was also unclear how the farms would be distributed, as INTA was said to favour smaller, individual plots while Girón preferred collective plots or cooperatives, arguing that small plots would inevitably be sold to larger farmers or be lost to banks in loan foreclosures.[27] However, local analysts pointed out the serious drawbacks of any type of land bank scheme (see box, pages 100-1): the land would be exorbitantly expensive for peasants to buy and would result in their being heavily dependent on outside loans for long periods; it would only benefit a small percentage of the landless and land-poor peasantry; some of the land was either run-down and therefore in need of considerable amounts of time and technical support, or located in areas where conflict with local peasants was likely (as had already happened in Yepocapa); and it was uncertain whether Girón's movement or the INTA-sponsored groups were controlled by the leadership or the rank-and-file. Cynics argued that although the scheme was at least a recognition of the land problem, it was more beneficial to Cerezo's populist credentials and to the banks' liquidity than to the vast numbers of *campesinos* in desperate need of land. In short, they maintained that the scheme was only a temporary

---

Land Options in Guatemala

Previous Options:
1) Arbenz's Agrarian Reform, 1952 – 54 (AID estimates):
Area affected: *884,000 hectares*, of which 604,000 were expropriated, and 280,000 were public land.
Number of beneficiaries: *Between 78,000 and 100,000 peasants,* i.e. between 31 and 40 per cent of the landless labour force.

2) Land Titling Programme, 1955 – 1982 (AID estimates):
Area affected: *665,000 hectares*, of which 66 per cent was frontier land.
Number of Beneficiaries: *50,000 families*, between 3.5 and 8.9 per cent of the landless, depending on the period.

Options for 1986:
The Demand: In 1982 AID estimated that there were 420,000 landless agricultural workers in Guatemala — since then, the figure has probably risen. Taking the AID-estimated 3.5 hectares of non-irrigated land that is the maximum that can be cultivated efficiently by one family, and the INTA 7-hectare estimate, they would need between 1.5 million and 3 million hectares of land.

Possible Available Land:
1) 1,200,000 hectares (Idle private land — AID estimate)
2) 369,000 hectares (Government land — AID)
3) 42,000 hectares (124 farms worth Q45 million available on private land market — INTA)
4) 18,000 hectares (29 farms worth Q7 million held by government or private banks — INTA) ▸

---

palliative, merely tinkering with a deeply unjust and ingrained land structure which demanded at the very least expropriation of the 3 million acres of idle privately owned land. As the box shows, President Arbenz's 1952 expropriatory agrarian reform benefited by far the most peasants in the shortest time span.

Predictably, Girón's movement was enough to send most of the agrarian élite into apoplexy, while the government's repeated rejection of agrarian reform was not enough to remove the mistrust many landowners still held for the Christian Democrat populist strand. The presence of Raquel de Blandón and the two government ministers at the July rally only confirmed their worst suspicions and provoked a rash of shrill TV and media advertising from UNAGRO, CACIF and their ilk. Girón was variously accused of being a hothead, of dividing the Guatemalan family and going beyond the proper concerns of the

Potential Beneficiaries: (using 7-hectare estimate)
Under 1): 171,000 families.
Under 2): 53,000 families.
Under 3): 6,000 families (or 18,000 families according to INTA).
Under 4): 2,500 families.

Source: Adapted from *Inforpress*, 19 June 1986.

The Potential Cost of a Land Bank Scheme:
1) Assuming Girón's movement has 50,000 family heads as members and 7 hectares per family, the movement would need 350,000 hectares. Assuming also an average price of Q1,100 per hectare, just to buy the 350,000 hectares would cost approximately Q400 million (or US$160 million). The 50,000 families represent around 10 per cent of those needing land.

2) According to INTA figures, government funds for purchasing farmland are limited to Q3 million, although Treasury Bonds may be issued for sale to raise additional funds.[1] The official commercial price of the *finca* at Yepocapa was Q1 million, considered artificially high, with the loan to be paid back within 10 years.[2]

3) The mortgages on the 23 farms formerly belonging to García Granados and sought by Girón's movement amounted to around US$110 million, way beyond the reach of Girón's supporters. When INTA explored the possibility of acquiring farms mortgaged to the Guatemalan banking system, the local banks frustrated INTA's inventory by quickly transferring these accounts to other financial entities.[3]

Sources: 1. *This Week*, 12 January 1987; 2. *This Week*, 8 December 1986; 3. *Inforpress*, 19 June 1986.

church. More seriously, he received a number of death threats, while the walls of his church buildings were festooned with red-painted insults and warnings.

The landowners' more reasoned response consisted of appealing to the highly controversial Article 39 of the new Constitution, which guaranteed private property rights. The new Constitution was more conservative than the four previous Constitutions, all of which had recognised the social function of property, and had been ratified only after allegations that nearly Q500,000 had 'circulated' in Congress in order that the phrase 'social function of property' should be excluded. Alternatively, the landowners argued that state lands should be used for such land handouts (despite the fact that the USAID study had shown that state land was not sufficient to solve the land problem and 30 years of land colonisation had produced no solutions for the vast majority of small producers); or they maintained that an agrarian reform inevitably led to sharp falls in agricultural production (despite the fact that vast amounts of private land were not even in production).

They also opposed the land bank scheme as a hidden form of expropriation because the land the peasants bought would be valued by the state and not by the market — they preferred that all available mortgaged land should instead be sold to the highest bidder, which would have effectively ruled out any peasant farmer. To many observers, the fundamental reason for the landowners' opposition was their fear that any distribution of land could eventually lead to the revival of Arbenz's famous Decree 900 which announced his agrarian reform programme in 1952. Such an extension of the policy could result in both the loss of some of their land and an inevitable reduction in the availability of the cheap labour on which their wealth depended.

Stability without Development

Cerezo could not adopt more radical polices like an agrarian reform, tax reform or nationalisation measures, because his economic and political strategy was based on engineering a consensus with the private sector similar to the one reached with the army. He was not tempted by the possibility of playing off CACIF against the army (which may have been feasible given their mutual animosity through 1985), but instead courted them both. The new government of course inherited the economic mess outlined in Chapter 1, but the social cost of the adjustment measures designed to stabilise the crisis was borne by the poorer sectors and not by the business class.

Cerezo's overall neo-liberal economic strategy — broadly, though not precisely, in agreement with IMF thinking — had three basic objectives: to bring down inflation by printing less money and relaxing price controls; to seek renewed economic growth by giving incentives for the private sector and foreign capital to invest and produce — without touching the dominant land and tax structure, but with special attention to traditional agro-exports and non-traditional exports through the Caribbean Basin Initiative; and to seek foreign aid to help solve the shortage of foreign exchange and balance of payments crisis. The policies were fundamentally geared towards securing the confidence and investment of the private sector but offered little hope of alleviating the social effects of the crisis.

The clumsily-titled Plan for Economic and Social Reordering (PRES), launched in June, was the cornerstone of the government strategy. The rhetoric that accompanied the PRES encouraged both labour and the private sector to work together, but the government clearly calculated that the weak and divided popular movement would offer much less resistance than the more unified and belligerent CACIF. In essence the plan favoured capital: it offered a bonanza of quetzals to the agro-exporters by allowing them to change their dollars at a new rate of US$1:Q2.50, when previously they had to work largely at a US$1:Q1.40 rate. With a new tax of 30 per cent on agro-exports the government hoped to reduce the Q400m fiscal deficit, but the net effect was windfall profits for the agro-exporters.[28] In fact, the government only managed to receive around 45 per cent of what they had planned from the agro-export tax, largely as a result of the fall in the price of coffee.[29] The removal of price ceilings on more than 300 basic consumer goods including soap, bread, powdered milk and especially maize was designed to bring down inflation by hopefully increasing supply and allowing the market to set the prices. A plan aimed at creating 40,000 emergency jobs in the public sector through the investment of Q100 million was the main measure to combat unemployment.

Contrary to the reception given to Mejía's 1985 proposals, the PRES won the temporary support of the business high command. It was the successful culmination of the rapprochement and strong ideological ties between the DCG and the more dynamic sectors within CACIF. Government functionaries Paiz (Finance Minister), Linares (President of the Central Bank) and Sosa (Minister of the Economy) were not only considered partisans of IMF-type solutions but also *'gente de ellos'* or 'CACIF's men'. The majority of the business community understood that the plan both favoured their interests and concurred with their free-market solution to the crisis in which the principal problem was not the distribution of wealth but insufficient production. Leonel Toriello, a leading figure within the Chamber of Industry, detected 'a remarkable change' in the receptivity of the government to business concerns, while Pedro Lamport, then CACIF's leader and chief negotiator, admitted that the programme 'hurt labour more than capital'.[30]

According to some conventional economic criteria, Cerezo's economic team did enjoy some success in stabilising the economy. Government figures for economic growth in 1986 registered 0.0 per cent (compared to -1.1 per cent in 1985) although private forecasters saw a further contraction of between 1 and 2 per cent.[31] The quetzal did recover some ground against the dollar, reaching Q2.50:US$1, although many argued that this was due less to the success of the PRES than to the temporary renegotiation of debt repayments, importers being able to buy their foreign exchange at the Q2.50:US$1 rate through the Central Bank, or the Bank of Guatemala's manipulating the foreign exchange markets in anticipation of an IMF demand for a unified exchange rate.[32] Foreign currency reserves rose from under US$8 million in 1985 to US$484 million by September 1986, although this was considerably aided by the depression in productive imports due to the amount of idle industrial capacity [33]. The downturn in oil prices and the temporary upturn in coffee prices also helped. In addition, around US$200 million in outstanding debt maturing in 1986 was rescheduled, although total debt service for the year amounted to just under US$500 million — a staggering 42 per cent of export earnings.[34]

The government also claimed success in reducing inflation from 31.5 per cent in 1985 to 25 per cent in 1986, but these figures were generally considered to be very conservative and to underestimate the rapid increase in food prices which ate away at the standard of living of the poor. The relaxation of price controls on basic food items failed to make any impact except upwards, as merchants continued to indulge in hoarding and speculation. Beans and maize, which make up half the basic diet of the 63 per cent of the population who live below the poverty line, and other basic food items continued to shoot up in price by between 30 and 100 per cent. Contrary to expectation, it was not the small producers who benefited from the price rises, but the intermediaries and merchants. For example, in the case of rice, Q25 a quintal was paid to the producer, but the price paid by the consumer was Q65 a quintal. Also, small-scale farmers were adversely affected by the 300 per cent rise in the price of fertilisers (from Q0.29 per hectare in 1985 to Q0.97 in early 1987), which was one factor behind the need for Guatemala to import 7.3m quintals of basic food items in 1986 (equivalent to over a quarter of total food production).[35] The lack of incentives for small producers was compounded by the excessive rains in the west of the country and the drought in the east. There was also increased demand for maize and beans as people turned to cheaper food in times of hardship. The result: in 1986 Guatemala was forced to import a staggering US$99 million worth of maize, beans and rice.

The rise in inflation might not have mattered so much if the wages of those in work had been rising correspondingly. The only significant pay increase awarded by the government to labour was a Q50 a month rise for state employees — almost certainly a politically necessary move to buy off the more organised workers. The Minister of Employment backtracked on an earlier promise for an enforced Q50 increase for private sector employees and minimum salary legislation, but instead gave in to CACIF's insistence that such measures would deter investment and therefore create more unemployment. Despite the inflation, wages remained fixed at 1980 levels, and instead the government made an 'act of faith' in CACIF's promise to grant wage increases voluntarily. There was considerable doubt as to how many of the country's 5,266 private firms actually stuck to their promise. Within a few days in July, the Minister for Employment, Catalina Soberanis, changed the figure of firms who had granted a wage increase from 882 to 4,648 — apparently to avoid the political risk of having to introduce a new legally enforced minimum wage.[36] In the 40 months prior to September 1986, labour suffered a 46 per cent drop in purchasing power — described by *Inforpress* as 'a fall in family income without comparison in modern Guatemalan history'. More than a third of that loss (16.7 per cent) had occurred since Cerezo took office in January.[37]

Nor was any headway made on reducing unemployment, as around half the population was still officially recognised as having no permanent job. There were even questions as to whether the Q100 million promised for job creation ever materialised. CEMLA (the Centre for Latin American Monetary Studies) estimated that by September only 20 per cent of the total Q600 million allocated to government investment in the 1986 budget — of which the Q100 million formed a part — had actually been spent.[38] In early 1987 the Ministry of Labour announced that only 8,000 of the planned 40,000 jobs had been created. The level of social services and health care remained catastrophic. The nation's health was not helped by the government's authorising a sharp price increase in basic medicine prices, some of which were said to have risen ten-fold in just three months from July to September.[39] According to the President of the Congress Health Commission, Carlos González, more than 200,000 cases of malaria were registered throughout the country in 1986, up from 10,000 the year before.[40]

Moreover, preliminary figures suggested that the government had failed in its key objective of getting the private sector to invest — in 1986 private investment shrank an additional 5.3 per cent from previous years to its lowest level for two decades.[41] Part of the reason for this may have been due to the government's engagement of the Geneva-based private firm, the Société Générale de Surveillance (SGS). The SGS started work in August in an attempt to crack down on various fraudulent private sector trading practices such as the under- and over-invoicing of imports and exports, which Linares himself declared cost the country as much as one-third of the annual value of its exports.[42] Various business groups complained that the SGS caused major administrative delays to their exports and was one step away from state control of foreign trade. To its credit, the government did not back down. Cerezo argued that those who opposed the SGS were the same people who for many years had tucked away more than US$2 billion abroad through such practices.

The private sector was also mistrustful of the government's tentative new tax plans, although these were always designed to combat evasion and increase the amount of tax that should be paid rather than change the highly regressive tax structure. Edgar Pappe, the progressive vice-Minister of Finance, had planned substantial increases in direct taxation, changes to make banks and insurance companies liable and new taxes on luxury goods. He also promised tougher action on evasion as he estimated only 25 per cent of tax due to the state was actually paid. Unsurprisingly, Pappe was disliked by business and dismissed.[43] In October the Agriculture Minister, Estrada, announced the predicted new tax on idle land, which was followed in November by the announcement of a packet of new tax measures. Again, none of the November measures, even if they were ever successfully implemented, altered the tax structure — the rate remained the same whatever the income — but on the contrary hit the low and medium income earners the hardest.[44]

By the end of the year the private sector was not totally satisfied, but was nevertheless not actively opposed to the new government. For the moment it was happy with the stabilisation plan but in the long term it was worried by the lack of definition of the exact role the state would play in the future of the economy. Ideologically, of course, the private sector remained opposed to any policy that implied strong action by the state, which it argued could be better performed by private capital. It was therefore still mistrustful of the 'developmentalist' leanings of some members of the government and the ideological ties with army officers closest to them, who obviously favoured more money for their social programmes, which, if abandoned, could benefit the left. The private sector's uncertainty was shared by other observers, who failed to see any clear-cut resolution to the problems of who would administer or control the development poles, and secondly whether the hitherto small amounts of government money directed towards public investment and the development poles would be increased.[45] The real losers were the thousands of Indians living in the model villages and development poles, which clearly admitted nothing more than the physical survival of their inhabitants. As the 1987 Americas Watch/British PHRG report observed:

> With the election of a civilian government, the Army has stopped supplying food and building materials in many communities, stating that it is the government's responsibility. The civilian government is not able to

meet the need, however, and hunger, disease and unemployment are common.[46]

The Radical Abroad

Foreign aid was the final ingredient in Cerezo's programme of economic recovery, and a foreign policy of 'active neutrality' in the region was a central mechanism for securing it. His unwillingness to confront the rich made new flows of aid even more urgent, both to help the balance of payments and to instigate development programmes in the rural areas. In his search for aid from Western European and Latin American sources, Cerezo was considerably helped by his support for the Contadora process (started in 1983 under the sponsorship of Mexico, Colombia, Venezuela, and Panama in an attempt to find a political solution to the regional conflict), his proposal for a Central American parliament, and his refusal to 'become an instrument of the US' or to condone Washington's support for the contras. Most Latin American and European governments welcomed Cerezo's overtures and policy for the advantages offered by a 'democratic' regional government supporting their own lukewarm efforts to seek a negotiated solution to the regional crisis.

In fact, Cerezo's 'active neutrality' was not a particularly innovative policy but a more high-profile pursuit of the Mejía regime's gentle non-alignment. Guatemala's neutrality had been deftly promoted by Fernando Andrade, Mejía's Foreign Minister, and stemmed not from any sympathy for the Sandinistas but from an astute recognition of the advantages of improved relations with Western European and Latin American countries (especially Mexico). It helped to reduce the country's international isolation, deflect criticisms of Guatemala's human rights record, and counter the level of international support for the URNG. Andrade's policy found plenty of support from the army. In part this was due to the military's fierce chauvinism and pique at the Carter administration's decision to cut them off from military aid in 1977, but they were also concerned not to divert their attention or troops away from their own civil war, and were generally disdainful of too close a collaboration with their military counterparts in Honduras and El Salvador.

For fiscal year (FY) 1986 US aid totalled US$104 million (nearly half for balance of payments support), while a further US$134 million was planned for 1987. In addition, Reagan's frequently-frustrated attempts to give significant amounts of official military aid to the Guatemalan army — although US$36 million worth of US tanks and US$7 million worth of US-made gunsights had gone in through the back door in 1982-4 [47] — were finally rewarded with Congress's approval of US\$5 million of military aid for 1986, with only US\$2 million earmarked for 1987. The US\$5 million was a modest sum when compared to the massive handouts given to the Honduran and Salvadorean armies, but it was significant because Cerezo himself was said to have asked for US\$1 million. This was interpreted by some as the Reagan administration deliberately courting the Guatemalan army as a way of increasing pressure on Cerezo, in order to force him to fall into line with US military dictates for Central America. Cerezo's aides spoke privately of fierce, even 'brutal', US opposition. Throughout 1986 Reagan also refused to invite Cerezo to the White House (in contrast to all the other Central American Presidents except Daniel Ortega of Nicaragua).

Top army officials did seem to be lending their ears to the offers of more aid. General Hernández, known for his good contacts with senior US military officers, warned publicly in November that Guatemala 'could change its neutrality because conditions are changing', and also spoke of looking forward to receiving more military aid from the US in 1987.[48] In the same month Captain Cifuentes, the armed forces spokesman, also ominously declared that active neutrality could change if Cerezo were to drop his present position and help the Tegucigalpa Bloc countries, Honduras, El Salvador and Costa Rica, who generally supported Reaganite positions.

The growing army, US and private sector pressure on Cerezo made it all the more important for him to diversify his sources of aid. This diversification was a key element of Cerezo's frequent visits abroad, the most publicised of which was to Europe in October. The net result of a whirlwind tour of Spain, France, Belgium, West Germany and Italy — the principal European exporters to Guatemala and the main importers of Guatemalan goods — was an estimated US\$300 million in loans and grants. He also won vital European support for his 'fragile democracy', notably from the Christian Democrat governments in West Germany and Italy. The renewal of diplomatic relations with Britain in December 1986 also brought offers of technical training scholarships from Baroness Young of the Foreign Office.

Despite Cerezo's commendable resistance to the assault on his 'active neutrality', there were clear limits on any positive application of the policy. After all, Cerezo was no supporter of the Sandinistas. He left West Germany with the declaration that 'in Central America there are four democracies and one totalitarian system, and it is the task of the democracies to contribute to the construction of democracy in Nicaragua', while he repeatedly told US government officials that at the end of the day they sat on the same side of the table.

Throughout the year, there were a number of incidents that seemed to undermine Guatemala's official position of neutrality: contra luminaries like Edén Pastora regularly appeared on TV, were interviewed in the press, and participated in round-table discussions. On one occasion, Adolfo Calero and two other contra leaders turned up in Guatemala City without any record of their entry into the country — it was suspected that they had flown in on a US military plane. The MLN was claiming that some 8,000 'Guatemalans' had been training in the east of the country to eventually join the contras (local observers thought it was more like a few hundred). In November the (still clandestine) PGT accused CACIF members of using a DC-123 to ferry supplies to the contras, and the CIA of contracting Guatemalan officers to train the contras. In the most publicised incident, the name of General Augusto Cáceres Rojas (assistant chief of staff under Mejía) appeared on an end-user certificate for 800 tons of mainly Portuguese arms that went to the contras as part of Colonel Oliver North's Irangate operations. Some of the arms were said to have been shipped while Cerezo was President.

But despite these and other incidents, most observers were agreed that Cerezo himself remained in favour of Guatemala's neutrality. In his words, he was not going to change his policy because the regionalisation of the war would mean an unacceptable rise in the defence budget, an increase in army recruitment, and the added danger of 'one bomb being enough to destroy the hydro-electric dam of Chixoy'.[49] He even added that 'if the Nicaraguan people chose a certain system of government, we should respect that decision, just as they should respect our chosen political system'.[50]

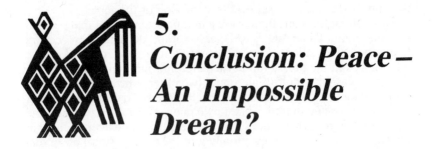

5.
Conclusion: Peace – An Impossible Dream?

'What's the good of five years of a civilian President if his only aim is to stay in office? Not to touch anything is hardly a solution. Cerezo is not consolidating civilian rule — he's consolidating a social and economic crisis.' Guatemalan journalist, July 1986.

To many human rights observers, politicians or governments based in Western Europe, Cerezo seems an attractive alternative to a military dictatorship. He offers not only a more realistic foreign policy of peace for the region, but also a serious 'option for peace' in Guatemala. Many Guatemalans voted for Cerezo as the best hope for peace and an end to the civil war, in much the same way that many Salvadoreans hoped that President Duarte would bring a peaceful resolution to the civil war in El Salvador. The Christian Democrat projects in both countries have manifestly failed to live up to their promises.

Throughout 1986 the incessant jingles on Guatemalan TV which sang of 'one more brick' being placed in the slow reconstruction of peace were a constant reminder of the government's objectives. Cerezo's strategy to achieve that peace was based on *concertación* or seeking consensus between all sectors of Guatemalan society. This consensus-building was both an embodiment of the fundamental Christian Democrat ideology that all sectors can be reconciled and work for the common good, and a clear indication of a sincere political and economic policy designed to pull Guatemala out of 30 years of acute political instability. But can it bring peace, and, if so, peace for whom?

Peace as an Absence of War?

During his trip to Europe in October 1986, Cerezo declared that he would be 'happy to talk with all sectors of the country, without prejudice of creed or ideology, in order to consolidate democracy, pluralism, and peace.'¹ The URNG immediately took up his offer, and suggested that top level talks could be held in the Spanish or Mexican embassies in Guatemala — or in Mexico — with the Spanish, French, German, Belgian or Italian government to vouch for the seriousness of the URNG offer. Cerezo refused on the grounds that the EGP, one of the members of the URNG, had recently captured and tortured seven military officials. The EGP's response was to declare that a number of soldiers were killed in combat, but to deny that they had tortured any soldier. Even if the EGP had engaged in torture, it was difficult to believe Cerezo's sincerity when the offices of Amnesty International are full of files detailing hundreds of acts of deliberate savagery carried out by the Guatemalan army. Cerezo added that the URNG could not be serious about its offer because 'it continued to carry out illegal and terrorist acts in the mountains'.

Later, in February 1987, the URNG offered a new basis for dialogue — their third attempt to start conversations since Cerezo took office. They proposed a six-point plan as a basis for discussions, which included a call for 'the largest and widest alliance in Guatemalan history to build democracy in Guatemala', a minimal programme of social reforms, an end to human rights violations and the humanisation of the war along the lines of the Geneva Convention. Cerezo again rejected their offer, arguing that he would only talk if they laid down their arms.²

Dialogue between the URNG and the Christian Democrat government may take place in the near future, although local analysts argue that the army may have vetoed any talks in return for their support for Cerezo. Although very unlikely, peace as 'the absence of fighting' may be achieved. But peace in the more positive sense of the removal of the structural causes that create the gross inequalities, the wrenching poverty and the horrendous human rights violations seems even more remote. It is hardly controversial to predict that without social reforms the URNG and the popular movement will inevitably recover their strength and once again offer a serious challenge to the status quo.

Peace — for One Year?

Cerezo enjoyed some temporary stability for his first year. He successfully engineered enough of a consensus with the traditional powerbrokers in Guatemala to ensure his political survival for the time being. Although events surrounding Nicaragua may decide Cerezo's political lifespan, loose agreements and ideological overlaps between the Christian Democrat government and more development-minded officers, and between the government and a more dynamic and modernising sector within CACIF, have been sufficient guarantees against a rapid return to direct military rule. But the price for staying in government has been that the poor have been left out of the process of *concertación*.

Real peace and stability in Guatemala have to be based on bringing solutions to the poverty of the majority and a reduction of the social and racial divide of which Chapters 1 and 2 are just a glimpse. To alleviate this poverty and social injustice any government in Guatemala can follow one of two courses: it can hope to attract enough investment from abroad and from the Guatemalan private sector to stimulate economic growth in the hope that the benefits of that growth may trickle down to the poor; it can hope to receive enough foreign aid to help balance of payments difficulties and bring some 'developmentalist' reforms to the countryside; and it can also introduce some mild reforms that do not fundamentally affect the frozen pattern of land or income distribution.

Alternatively, a government can implement 'policies of hope' — like those listed at the end of Chapter 1 — that go beyond the existing economic system and seriously affect the private sector; an expropriatory land reform which gives land to peasants, takes away some of the landowners' wealth and threatens their source of cheap labour; an overhaul of the tax system to allow the state to improve health, education, and infrastructure, while allowing less income for the wealthy few; nationalising the trading and banking sectors to allow the state to control the shortage of dollars and direct investment to more socially useful ends, and limit the profits of commercial and financial capital.

Cerezo has chosen the former path. The first year did bring some economic 'stability' as compared with the crisis Cerezo inherited, but the cost of the stability was clearly borne by the poor. The DCG government hoped that by giving enough guarantees of the privileges of the private sector it would stimulate investment. But it is a high risk strategy given the continued regional instability surrounding Nicaragua and El Salvador, and CACIF's lingering mistrust of Christian Democrat statist or developmentalist tendencies. Moreover, even if Cerezo is successful in getting the private sector and foreign capital to invest, the last 30 years of virtually untrammelled free enterprise economic 'development' have only accentuated social inequalities and kept the poor majority far removed from any benefits of economic growth.

Furthermore, the reforms which began to emerge by the end of the year — even if they are fully implemented — only tinker with the system: a land bank scheme instead of an agrarian reform; taxes on idle land and property instead of the replacement of a hopelessly regressive tax structure; employing a private firm to control illegal import and export practices instead of nationalising foreign trade; and some 'developmentalist' programmes for war-torn areas that can be nothing more than palliatives.

In a highly polarised country like Guatemala where there are so few rich and so many poor, to turn to the few as major allies is bound to leave a government susceptible to the social explosion of the many. It is virtually impossible to defuse the acute social polarisation by giving little, or nothing, to the poor. The great unknown is whether the depth of the economic crisis will spark an explosion — perhaps similar to the spontaneous demonstrations that shook Guatemala City in September 1985, or perhaps sparked off by Girón's *campesino* movement. At the time of writing, Cerezo is considerably aided by the temporary weakness of the left and the popular movement, for many of whom Cerezo's peace is the peace of the dead. The URNG, though showing signs of increased actions in 1986, is still on the defensive, while the trade union and *campesino* sectors are, understandably, only carefully and slowly re-emerging after years of fierce repression. But very few are under any illusions: should they or the URNG recover more of their strength and once again become a powerful mass movement, the repressive apparatus — still completely intact — will be unleashed in full force and the cycle of bloody repression will repeat itself.

1986 — A Missed Opportunity?

Cerezo's apologists claim that he must be given more time before being judged. One year is clearly not enough to resolve Guatemala's gargantuan problems, especially when the space for the DCG was in part created by the military's supervision of the electoral process. Moreover, they argue, for Cerezo to confront the right too soon would be tantamount to constructing his own political funeral pyre. As Cerezo himself has posed the dilemma, 'if we institute reform measures that affect the private sector, and don't take the army into account, we shall be overthrown; and if we attack the army without having the business sector on our side, the result would be the same.' But Cerezo had a historic opportunity to break with the past, which he lost soon after the elections. In contrast, President Alfonsín in Argentina initially used a similar amount of electoral support to boldly push through the trial and imprisonment of some senior military officers, while Alan García in Peru used his popular majority to stand up to the might of the IMF and western banks as a way of beginning to tackle Peru's poverty.

A year is a sufficient period of time to evaluate the general direction of the new government. Even if the social reforms that are ultimately the solution for the poor majority are ruled out by contemporary political reality, the vast majority of the policies in the first year clearly favoured the powerful. There was no minimum wage legislation; there were no price ceilings, no serious human rights investigations or dismantling of the security apparatus, and no significant tax changes. The land bank idea may seem like a step in the right direction, but there are serious doubts about its costs, the predictable bureaucratic delays, and the number of potential beneficiaries. In short, Cerezo seems not just unable, but unwilling, to confront the right, nor has he turned to the popular sectors to bolster himself against them. Although the Christian Democrat government presents itself as an autonomous political option, the result so far has been that the 'democratic opening' has been far more useful to CACIF and the army than to the poor. CACIF has been guaranteed most of its privileges. The army has been given a means to consolidate and legitimise its counter-insurgency programmes. The poor get next to nothing.

Peace through the Third Way?

Although for the moment the Christian Democrat Party is placed firmly on the right of the political spectrum, in time it may return to a more centrist position, seeking a third way between the 'extremes' of the traditional military-oligarchy alliance and revolution. But it is doubtful whether even a centrist DCG could bring stability to the country, an end to the human rights violations, or lasting solutions to the poor.

The 'democratic opening' and the new government have brought with them more space for popular organisation and protest. In part this stems from the need for the DCG to rebuild an organised popular base — especially amongst trade unions or peasants — such as it enjoyed in the 1960s and early 1970s. Although there are few signs that this has been a major priority for the new government, in the medium term the DCG must do this both for its own political ends, and to act as a more stable political option for those sectors of the army, the private sector and the US government who can see the advantages of more 'consensual' formulas for tempering social polarisation and isolating the revolutionary left.

However, the tension between the need for space for a DCG popular base and the need for state violence to maintain the economic status quo is bound in the long run to be resolved in favour of the latter. If the DCG make serious attempts to set up an independent power base, they would have no mechanism for controlling any process of wider popular mobilisation. Although at present a more 'developmentalist' strand within the Guatemalan army may be in the ascendant, this does not mean that the army will not happily return to more uncomplicated forms of social control if the need arises. It remains fiercely imbued with an anti-communism that interprets dissent as subversion (and is frequently used as an excuse by the military to stay in power), and sees popular organisation as a Cuban-backed threat to national security. As long as the army remains untouchable and free from prosecution, human rights violations will inevitably continue.

The question of human rights violations is also inescapably linked to the unwillingness of the new government to confront the private sector and introduce wider social reforms. Recent Guatemalan history has shown that the people who have wealth and power in the country are prepared to defend it with extraordinary violence by disappearing, killing or massacring those who are fighting to change, however moderately, the systems that guarantee that wealth. *Campesinos* and workers who form cooperatives or unions, Indians who join or support — or frequently are merely suspected of supporting — guerrilla movements, and mothers who claim the right to know what happened to their relatives have been the victims of death squads or army savagery. The Guatemalan families who own the land, the capital and the businesses are some of the most extreme and unyielding in the hemisphere, sincerely believing that only an unfettered free market economy can permit them high profits, which in turn would generate more investment and therefore more jobs. In the past right-wing elements within the private sector have been prepared to defend savagely their chosen economic model and their priveleges. If seriously challenged, they are unlikely to surrender any of their economic power without a fight.

A middle path brings with it contradictions that inevitably lead to periods of more acute social polarisation. Where will the DCG stand? In the past the party has shown itself only too willing to turn to CACIF, the army and the US rather than to the poor for its political survival. One poor *campesino* at the July rally in Nueva Concepción expressed the unavoidable choice Cerezo had to face: 'Is he on the side of the same groups who have dominated my country for the last 30 years — or is he with us?'

Appendix: Communities in Resistance

Interview with Mateo, a Chuj Indian, October 1986

Let me tell you how the communities in resistance began. The story goes back to the 1960s, around then, when the church began to set up rural cooperatives in isolated areas, Ixcán and across the Northern Transversal Strip. There were five of these cooperatives in a project run by the Huehuetenango diocese. Many of us, families from the poorest sectors of our country, went up to join the cooperatives after years of migrating to the coast, to work in the coffee and cotton plantations and to cut cane.

The independent rural cooperatives
We settled on the cooperatives, and as time went by our crops developed and we improved our standard of living. We were able to get hold of some livestock — cattle and other animals — and we grew coffee, cardamom, sugar, lots of other crops. The Catholic priests helped us to get advice on agriculture from agronomists. And with the aid of the church we built schools, a church, a market. Because of the isolation, one of the first jobs for each cooperative was to build an airstrip for small planes, and this was our only communications link, to transport our products to the nearest town and to bring back things we needed in our community, and also to get people out if they were ill or hurt in an accident. The planes belonged to the church and had been obtained through the parish priest who was working with us. The pilots were volunteers.

In the area there was another project, run by INTA, the government's Agrarian Transformation Institute. We struck up a relationship with the peasants in that project. They visited us, we told them about our experiences and how we had formed the cooperatives, and they organised themselves into cooperatives as well. This made a total of 17 cooperatives, and a managing committee was formed for all of them.

With the formation of the other cooperatives, we were forging ahead. There were also parish schools, and the church set up courses to train health promoters. Also, each cooperative had a shop — not the kind of shop where one person exploits all the rest, but a community store where everybody bought and sold produce at the same price, with no-one making a profit out of it. So in fact we were pretty content, because after all those years of suffering working down on the coast, we had our crops, our animals. Yes, we were content.

The wolf descends on the fold

But when the government and the army realised the kind of development we were carrying out, they started to crack down. In 1978 they killed the parish priest who was working with us. The next priest was soon expelled from the country. So were the pilots. They stopped our flights, so we were left with no way of getting our produce out or of bringing in the things we needed. The army said they'd run the flights for us and bring things in and out. But three, four months went by, six months, and there'd been not one flight for our produce or for our sick people. So we began to approach government institutions, asking them to run the flights for us as they'd promised, because it was vitally important to us. We travelled all the way to the capital to put our case, but the treatment we got was disgraceful, complete contempt, as if we weren't people at all. In fact, our cooperatives were supplying Huehue-tenango and Quiché, but the army prevented us from doing this, and the villages suffered too, because their food wasn't getting through to them. But when we complained to the government institutions, they called us subversives.

From then on the army began to repress us. Cooperative members started to disappear. People would be killed at night in their cottages, women were raped, the cooperative shops were robbed, and afterwards the army would say it was the guerrillas who had done it. But our people knew otherwise. As the repression grew, we lost any respect we might have had for the army. When we held our monthly or yearly meetings, army people took control and decided what would be done. We were no longer free to discuss, to plan, to decide on our actions cooperatively. They ran the meetings, not us.

It was in January or February of 1982 that the army began to raze our crops, burn down our houses, kill our animals, and massacre women, children, and old people completely without mercy. The first massacre was in the community of Cuarto Pueblo on 14 March 1982. More than 300 people were killed in a market — the army surrounded them under cover of night and right there they machine-gunned them all. Other massacres followed. We fled into the mountains with our families and whatever we could carry. Because in the end they did away with everything, shops, storehouses, schools, markets, clinics, everything in the community, even down to the animals. So we had to take refuge in the mountains, even though we had no experience of living rough.

That was during 1982. Throughout 1983, they followed us into the mountains. Again they destroyed our crops, the little that we'd been able to build, our little straw huts, and the few things we'd been able to rescue out of the villages and communities. In that year we suffered terribly. We were without food, without clothes, without shelter, exposed to rain, sun, the chill of the night. Out of pure need, we had to eat the berries off the trees, the berries the animals eat, and that helped us to survive. We discovered some roots that we could eat. These were things we'd never eaten before — out of sheer hunger, we discovered plants that helped us survive.

All that year we kept meeting other groups of people wandering in the mountains, who had fled from other places. We met up, and since we already had experience of cooperative living, we joined up with them. But as soon as we joined up in groups of 150, 200 families, the army would track us down; they could trace us by the noise a large group of people makes.

At the end of that year we met to discuss what to do. Many families had gone into exile in Mexico, but we didn't want to do that — to leave our land, our little plots, our country. If we went to Mexico, we knew we'd be subject to the Mexican authorities. But we refused to join the civil patrols either. We knew the army's ways: they'd killed our relatives and smashed everything it had cost us so much to achieve. We decided we would prefer to live in the mountains, however great the hardship, than to submit to the control either of the Guatemalan army or of the Mexican authorities. So since then we have been living in resistance in the mountains.

Tactics for survival

We formed a committee, called the Provisional Committee of Smallholders of Ixcán, and started to look for ways of getting in touch with the other communities round about. After the attacks we'd suffered from the army when we were in big groups, we decided to scatter throughout the mountains in lots of little groups, groups of 25 to 30 families so that we could move about more quickly and escape faster when the army came. And with the Committee, with everyone carrying out their particular task, we could also communicate quickly with nearby communities.

We'd learned a lot during 1982-83. We'd had experience of how to defend ourselves from attack by the army, from bombing and machine-guns. So we organised production better, and look-outs. We learned what kinds of root vegetables to plant — *malanga*, for example, which is a plant whose stem and leaf you can eat. It keeps us alive when the army cuts down our cornfields or our rice and beans. You can eat it with or without salt — as a staple food and as a herb. It's easy to grow and the army doesn't notice it from the air because it blends in with the undergrowth. Whereas with corn, rice and beans, the army can see them at a distance from a plane or helicopter. Another way of protecting what we have planted is to plant in different places. In the first years, when we planted a crop all in one place, the army cut it all down. So the solution was to plant in various places, not just one. This has been quite successful. We've also learned not to stay too long in any one place; every so often we move on.

So we've begun to grow again. Education is organised for the children, and training courses for teachers. At the moment we're managing to teach up to fourth grade, and this year [1986] we began a literacy campaign with adults. It's the same with health care: there are courses to train community health workers. Each community in resistance has a person responsible for health care. We have discovered the uses of several herbs and roots, and this is useful because bought medicines, industrially produced medicines, are not enough and are difficult to obtain. Most people use medicinal plants.

Out of the years of suffering and persecution by the army, we've created new forms of self-defence. We organise a system of look-outs, setting up guardposts around the communities and around the crops when we're working. When those on watch see the army coming and give warning, we leave our huts and the whole community runs away. When the army get there they burn and destroy the huts and all our possessions, any clothes and utensils they find, as well as our cornfields and vegetable gardens. When they go away again — we can tell when they return to their bases — then we also return, and rebuild.

Unity forged in hardship

Well, that's what life is like for us in the mountains. And I want to say that we're not just two or three families, we're hundreds of families, not only in Huehuetenango but in parts of Quiché. We're in close contact with each other. Together we form the Community of the People in Resistance. But we are all peasants. We are not armed, as the army or the government say. Most of us are indigenous people. We are peasants, women, children, old people, people left widowed or orphaned by army massacres.

We come from various ethnic groups — Mam, Kanjobal, Chuj, Cakchiquel, Kekchí — and there are also a few *ladinos*. But we've all learned to care for each other, to defend each other, and to live together. This life we lead in the mountains has taught us to live truly as persons, as human beings, and has given us a spirit of struggle. Our affection for each other, our love for our land and for our country, have enabled us to confront this situation which the army has imposed on us. We feel that if there is any democracy in Guatemala, it's here, for here we are free to express our opinions, both men and women. Women play an important role in our assemblies, and there are two women comrades on our committee at present. Women participate too in the local committees in each community. We believe women's participation is a seed of the new society.

We also feel in unity with our brothers and sisters in the groups waging the popular struggle — because we are familiar with exactly the same situation that they face. At the same time we sympathise with our brothers and sisters who are refugees in Mexico, because we can also imagine the situation they're in. So, for all those reasons, we don't feel alone, we feel part of the popular struggle here in Guatemala. And that gives us confidence; we're sure that with unity and with the support of the solidarity movement abroad we can bring about change in our country. We believe this life we are leading in the mountains is the birth of a new society.

Further Reading

Americas Watch/British Parliamentary Human Rights Group, *Human Rights in Guatemala*, London, 1987. Available from CIIR.

T. Barry and D. Preusch, *The Central America Fact Book*, Grove Press, New York, 1986.

P. Berryman, *Christians in Guatemala's Struggle*, CIIR, London 1984.

G. Black, *Under the Gun*, NACLA Report, November – December 1985.

CIIR, *Guatemala — Comment*, London, 1987.

J. Handy, *Gift of the Devil*, Between the Lines, Toronto, 1984.

Inforpress Centroamericana, *Guatemala 1986 — The year of promises*, Guatemala City, 1987.

Rigoberta Menchú, *I...Rigoberta*, ed. Elizabeth Burgos-Debray, Verso Books, London, 1984.

A. Nairn and J.M. Simon, 'The Bureaucracy of Death', *New Republic*, 30 June 1986.

R.G. Williams, *Export Agriculture and the Crisis in Central America*, University of North Carolina Press, 1986.

WOLA, *Without Security or Development: Guatemala Militarised*, Washington DC, 1985.

Periodicals:

Caribbean Insight, Box 100, 48 Albermarle Street, London W1.

Central America Report, Central America Human Rights Coordination, 83 Margaret Street, London W1.

Inforpress Centroamericana, 9a Calle 'A' 3-56, zone 1, Guatemala City.

Guatemala Briefing, Central America Information Service, 1 Amwell Street, London EC1R 1UL.

Abbreviations

AGA	*Asociación Guatemalteca de Agricultores*/Guatemalan Agriculturalists Association.
AIFLD	American Institute for Free Labor Development.
ANC	*Asociación Nacional Campesina Pro-Tierra*/National Peasant Association for Land.
ANACAFE	*Asociación Nacional del Café*/National Coffee Association.
ASAZGUA	*Asociación de Azucareros*/Sugar-Growers Association.
BANVI	*Banco Nacional de la Vivienda*/National Housing Bank.
CACIF	*Comité Coordinador de Asociaciones Agrícolas, Comerciales, Industriales y Financieras*/Chamber of Agriculture, Commerce, Industry and Finance.
CACM	Central American Common Market.
CAEM	*Cámara Empresarial*/Chamber of Business.
CAN	*Central Auténtica Nacionalista*/Authentic Nationalist Central.
CBI	Caribbean Basin Initiative.
CGTG	*Coordinadora General de Trabajadores Guatemaltecos*/General Coordination of Guatemalan Workers.
CLAT	*Confederación Latinoamericana de Trabajadores*/Latin American Workers Confederation.
CNT	*Central Nacional de Trabajadores*/National Workers Confederation.
CNUS	*Comité Nacional de Unidad Sindical*/National Committee for Trade Union Unity.
CRN	*Comité de Reconstrucción Nacional*/National Reconstruction Committee.
CUC	*Comité de Unidad Campesina*/Committee for Peasant Unity.
CUSG	*Confederación de Unidad Sindical de Guatemala*/Confederation of Guatemalan Trade Union Unity.
DCG	*Democracia Cristiana Guatemalteca*/Guatemalan Christian Democrat Party.

DIT	*Departamento de Investigaciones Técnicas*/Department of Technical Investigations.
EGP	*Ejército Guerrillero de los Pobres*/Guerrilla Army of the Poor.
FAR	*Fuerzas Armadas Rebeldes*/Rebel Armed Forces.
FCG	*Federación Campesina de Guatemala*/Guatemalan Peasant Federation.
FDCR	*Frente Democrático Contra la Represión*/Democratic Front Against Repression.
FDR/FMLN	*Frente Democrático Revolucionario/Farabundo Martí para la Liberación Nacional*/Democratic Revolutionary Front/Farabundo Martí National Liberation Front.
FECETRAG	*Federación Central de Trabajadores de Guatemala*/ Central Federation of Guatemalan Workers.
FEDECOCAGUA	*Federación de Cooperativas Cafetaleras de Guatemala*/ Guatemalan Federation of Coffee Cooperatives.
FESC	*Frente Estudiantil Social Cristiano*/Social Christian Student Front.
FNO	*Frente Nacional de Oposición*/National Opposition Front.
FTN	*Franja Transversal del Norte*/Northern Transversal Strip.
FUNDAP	*Fundación para el Desarrollo Integral de Programas Socio-económicos*/Foundation for the Integrated Development of Socio-economic Programmes.
FUNDESA	*Fundación para el Desarrollo*/Foundation for Development.
FUR	*Frente Unido de la Revolución*/United Front of the Revolution.
GAM	*Grupo de Apoyo Mutuo*/Mutual Support Group.
IDB	Inter-American Development Bank.
IDESAC	*Instituto para el Desarrollo Económico y Social de América Central*/Institute for the Economic and Social Development of Central America.
IGSS	*Instituto Guatemalteco de Seguridad Social*/Guatemalan Social Security Institute.
IICs	*Coordinadoras Interinstitucionales*/Inter-Institutional Coordination System.
ILO	International Labour Office.
IMF	International Monetary Fund.
INCAP	*Instituto de Nutrición de Centro América y Panamá*/ Institute for Nutrition in Central America and Panama.
INTA	*Instituto Nacional de Transformación Agraria*/National Institute for Agrarian Transformation.
IPM	*Instituto de Previsión Militar*/Military Social Welfare Institute.

MLN	*Movimiento de Liberación Nacional*/National Liberation Movement.
MONAP	*Movimiento Nacional de Pobladores*/National Slum-dwellers Movement.
NACLA	North American Congress on Latin America.
PDCN	*Partido Democrático de Cooperación Nacional*/ Democratic Party of National Cooperation.
PGT	*Partido Guatemalteco de Trabajadores*/Guatemalan Labour Party (also known as the Guatemalan Communist Party).
PID	*Partido Institucional Democrático*/Democratic Institutional Party.
PNR	*Partido Nacional Renovador*/National Renovation Party.
PR	*Partido Revolucionario*/Revolutionary Party.
PRA	*Partido Revolucionario Auténtico*/Authentic Revolutionary Party.
PRES	*Plan de Reordenamiento Económico y Social*/Plan for Economic and Social Reordering.
PSD	*Partido Socialista Democrático*/Social Democrat Party.
SEGEPLAN	*Secretaría General del Consejo Nacional de Planificación Económica*/State Planning Council.
TNC	Transnational Company.
UCN	*Unión del Centro Nacional*/Union of the National Centre.
UNAGRO	*Unión Nacional de Agricultores*/National Union of Agriculturalists.
UNSITRAGUA	*Unión Sindical de Trabajadores de Guatemala*/Trade Union Unity of Guatemalan Workers.
URNG	*Unidad Revolucionaria Nacional Guatemalteca*/ Guatemalan National Revolutionary Unity.
USAC	*Universidad de San Carlos*/National University of San Carlos.
USAID	United States Agency for International Development.
WOLA	Washington Office on Latin America.

Notes

Chapter 1: A Wealth of Poverty

1. UNICEF, *Dimensions of Poverty in Latin America and the Caribbean*, Washington DC, 1982.
2. Dirección General de Estadísticas, *Encuesta Nacional de Ingresos y Gastos Familiares*, Guatemala City, 1980-1, and additional calculations by SEGEPLAN.
3. INCAP/SEGEPLAN, *Regionalización de Problemas Nutricionales en Guatemala*, Guatemala City, 1980.
4. Quoted in *IXQUIC*, Mexico City, 6 October 1986.
5. Cited in C. D. Brockett, 'Malnutrition, Public Policy and Agrarian Change in Guatemala', *Journal of InterAmerican Studies and World Affairs*, November 1984, p.479.
6. *La Hora*, Guatemala City, 9 July 1986.
7. USAID, *Tierra y Trabajo en Guatemala*, Guatemala City, 1982.
8. Washington Office on Latin America (WOLA), *The Roots of Revolution*, Washington DC, 1983, p.4.
9. Dirección General de Servicios de Salud (DGSS) and Ministerio de Salud Pública y Asistencia Social (MSPAS), *Unidad de Informática*, Guatemala City.
10. MSPAS, *Memoria de Labores*, Guatemala City, 1986.
11. Dianna Melrose, *The Threat of a Good Example*, Oxford, 1985 p.18.
12. MSPAS, *Evaluación Plan Operativo 1985*, Guatemala City, 1986.
13. Guatemala Health Rights Support Project, *Guatemala: Health Care and Hope*, Washington DC, 1985, p.2.
14. WOLA, *op.cit*, p.4.
15. *Ibid*, p.4.
16. UN University, *Case Studies in Health-seeking Behaviour in Central America 1982-3*, Principal researcher: Hernán Delgado, INCAP.
17. *This Week* (Guatemala City), 10 March 1986 and *Inforpress* (Guatemala City), 26 June 1986.
18. Ministry of Public Finance figures, Guatemala City, various years.
19. A. Hintermeister, *Rural Poverty and Export Farming in Guatemala*,

International Labour Office, Geneva, 1984, p.7.
20. Guatemalan Human Rights Commission, *El Niño Guatemalteco en la Coyuntura Actual*, Mexico City, 1986, p.11.
21. *This Week*, 5 January 1987.
22. Author's interview, Guatemala, June 1986.
23. Carol Smith, 'Local History in Global Context: Social and Economic Transitions in Western Guatemala', *Comparative Studies in Society and History*, April 1984, p.206.
24. A. Hintermeister, *op.cit.*, p.11.
25. National Agrarian Censuses for 1950, 1964 and 1979, Guatemala City.
26. USAID, *Report of the AID Field Mission in Guatemala*, Guatemala City 1980.
27. S. Barraclough and P. Marchetti in *Towards An Alternative for Central America and the Caribbean*, eds. G. Irvin and X. Gorostiaga, Allen and Unwin, London, 1985, p.177.
28. WOLA, *op.cit.*, p.2.
29. Inforpress, *Guatemala: Elections 1985*, Guatemala City, October 1985, p.19.
30. ASIES, *El Sector Agropecuario: Eje de una Política de Reactivación Económica y Desarrollo Nacional*, Guatemala City, 1986, p.6.
31. USAID, *op.cit.*.
32. *Financial Times*, 12 December 1985.
33. Author's interview, Guatemala City, July 1986.
34. Piero Gleijeses, *The Struggle for Democracy*, University College, Cork, 1986, p.7.
35. USAID *op.cit.*, and A. Hintermeister, *op.cit.*
36. Jim Handy, *Gift of the Devil*, Between the Lines, Toronto, 1984, p.207.
37. R. E. Ortiz Rosales, 'Guatemala: Generalidades sobre el Sector Agrícola', *Comercio Exterior*, Mexico City, November 1984, p.1124.
38. PREALC, *Guatemala: Pobreza Rural y Crédito Agrícola al Campesino*, Santiago, 1985, p.33.
39. WOLA, *op.cit.*, p.5.
40. S. Barraclough and P. Marchetti, *op.cit.*, p.177-8.
41. IDB, *Economic and Social Progress in Latin America*, Washington DC, 1978, pp.138-141.
42. S.Barraclough and P.Marchetti, *op.cit.*, p.160.
43. A.Hintermeister, *op.cit.*, p.15.
44. ASIES, *op.cit.*, p.7.
45. WOLA, *op.cit.*, p.7.
46. A.Hintermeister, *op.cit.*, p.17.
47. *Inforpress*, 19 June 1986.
48. Inforpress, *Guatemala: Elections 1985*, Guatemala City 1985, pp.13 ff.
49. *Ibid*, p.14.
50. ASIES, *op.cit.*, p.10.
51. *El Día*, Guatemala City, 26 February 1986, quoting USAC figures.
52. Author's interview, Guatemala, June 1986.
53. *Prensa Libre*, Guatemala City, 30 August 1986.

54. *Inforpress*, 6 November 1986.
55. Author's interview, Guatemala, June 1986.
56. *This Week*, 5 August 1985.
57. *National Agrarian Census 1979*, Guatemala City.
58. Americas Watch, *Civil Patrols in Guatemala*, New York, 1986, p.7.
59. British Parliamentary Human Rights Group, *Bitter and Cruel*, London 1984, ch.3.
60. WOLA, *Without Security or Development: Guatemala Militarised*, Washington DC, 1985, p.27.
61. Author's interview, Guatemala City, June 1986.
62. Americas Watch, *op.cit.*, p.8.
63. Inforpress, *Guatemala: Elections 1985*, p.19.
64. PREALC, *op.cit.*, pp.49-50. and S. Barraclough and P. Marchetti, *op.cit.*, *passim.*
65. Inforpress, *op.cit.*, p.19, and T. Barry and D. Preusch, *The Central America Fact Book*, Grove Press, New York, 1986, p.160.
66. WOLA, *op.cit.*, pp.80-1.
67. Inforpress, *op.cit.*, p.19.

Chapter 2: A Separate World

1. *New York Times*, 3 August 1985.
2. For the source of this concept, see J. F. Petras and M. H. Morley, in *Revolution and Intervention in Central America*, eds. M. Dixon and S. Jonas, Synthesis, San Francisco, 1983, pp.190-1.
3. World Bank, *Guatemala: Country Economic Memorandum*, Washington DC, 1980.
4. T. Barry and D. Preusch, *The Central America Fact Book*, Grove Press, New York, 1986, p.243.
5. Minority Rights Group report no. 62, *Central America's Indians*, London, 1984, p.11.
6. Washington Office on Latin America, *Guatemala: The Roots of Revolution*, Washington DC, 1983, p.7.
7. *El Gráfico*, Guatemala City, 6 July 1986.
8. T. Barry, B.Wood and D.Preusch, *Dollars and Dictators*, The Resource Center, Albuquerque 1982, p.23.
9. *The Central America Fact Book*, p.146.
10. USAC, *El Cultivo del Café en Guatemala*, Guatemala City, 1981, p.vi.
11. USAC, *op.cit.*, chs. IV and V, *passim.*
12. *This Week*, 30 June 1986 and 15 September 1986.
13. *Financial Times*, 23 January 1986.
14. *Coffee and Cocoa International*, Issue 2, 1986, p.17.
15. British Parliamentary Human Rights Group, *Bitter and Cruel*, London, October 1984, p.29.
16. *La Palabra*, Guatemala City, 15 July 1986.
17. R.G.Williams, *Export Agriculture and the Crisis in Central America*,

University of North Carolina Press, 1986, p.51.
18. CEPAL, *América Latina y la Economía Mundial del Algodón*, Santiago 1985, p.87.
19. J.A. Figueroa Gálvez, *El Cultivo Capitalista del Algodón*, USAC, Guatemala City, 1980, p.22.
20. CEPAL, *op.cit.*, p.92.
21. R. Harris and C.Vilas (eds.), *Revolution Under Siege*, Zed, London, 1985, p.15.
22. CEPAL, *op.cit.*, p.87.
23. R.G.Williams, *op.cit.*, p.46.
24. The material on the Ponciano family is taken from a detailed study of the area around Tiquisate, carried out by a team of religious researchers. The title and authors cannot be printed for security reasons.
25. PREALC, *Guatemala: Pobreza Rural y Crédito Agrícola al Campesino*, Santiago, 1985, p.54.
26. *Inforpress*, 6 November 1986.
27. CEPAL, *op.cit.*, p.90.
28. J.A. Figueroa Gálvez, *op.cit.*, p.53.
29. Banco de Guatemala, *Informe Económico*, Guatemala City, April-June 1983, p.21.
30. *Inforpress*, 6 November 1986.
31. *South* (London), January 1985, p.73.
32. *Ibid*, p.73.
33. Roger Plant, *Guatemala: Unnatural Disaster*, Latin America Bureau, London, 1978, p.82.
34. NACLA, *Guatemala*, New York, 1974, pp. 213 ff.
35. S. Schlesinger and S.Kinzer, *Bitter Fruit*, Sinclair Browne, London 1982, p.238.
36. *Inforpress*, 19 June 1986.
37. *This Week*, 8 September 1986.
38. R.G.Williams, *op.cit.*, p.151.
39. *ibid.*, p.149.
40. L. Frank and P. Wheaton, *Indian Path to Liberation*, EPICA, Washington DC, 1984, p.55.
41. R.G.Williams, *op.cit.*, p.102.
42. Author's interview, July 1986.
43. *This Week*, 14 July 1986.
44. *This Week*, 10 March 1986.
45. NACLA, *Under the Gun*, November-December 1985, p.14.
46. *The Central America Fact Book*, p.244.
47. *This Week*, 22 April 1985.
48. George Black, *Garrison Guatemala*, Zed, London, 1984, p.58.
49. G. Paz Cárcamo, *Política Agraria: Una Propuesta para la Coyuntura de Guatemala en 1986*, ICADIS, Costa Rica, 1986, p.36, and Central American Historical Institute, *Update* no.82, Washington DC, 16 December 1985, p.1.
50. *This Week*, 3 February 1986.

51. Víctor Perera, 'Can Guatemala Change?', *New York Review of Books*, 14 August 1986, p.42.
52. *Proceso*, Mexico City, 16 September 1985.
53. *Caribbean Insight*, London, March 1986.
54. *Proceso*, *op.cit..*
55. J. L. Fried *et al.*, eds., *Guatemala in Rebellion*, Grove Press, New York, 1983, p.107.
56. *Inforpress*, 17 April 1986.
57. *Guatemala in Rebellion*, p.106.
58. WOLA, *op.cit.*, pp.3-4.
59. *The Central America Fact Book*, p.14.
60. Central American Historical Institute, *Update* no.82, Washington DC, 16 December 1985, p.2.
61. George Black, *op.cit.*, p.33.
62. NACLA, *Guatemala*, New York 1974, p.77.
63. *The Central America Fact Book*, pp.156-7.
64. *The Central America Fact Book*, p.247.
65. Economist Intelligence Unit (London), *Annual Survey of Central America*, London 1986, p.12.

Chapter 3: The Civilised Right

1. C. R. Montenegro Ríos, *El partido Demócrata Cristiano y su desarrollo político e ideológico*, MA thesis, University of Costa Rica, 1980, p.5.
2. T. Beeson and J. Pearce (eds.), *A Vision of Hope*, Fount Paperbacks, London, 1984, p.51.
3. Instituto de Investigaciones Políticas y Sociales (IIPS), *Los partidos políticos y el estado guatemalteco*, USAC, Guatemala City, 1978, p.32.
4. IIPS, *op.cit.*, p.35.
5. J. Handy, *Gift of the Devil*, Between the Lines, Toronto, 1984, p.213.
6. G. Gaspar, *La estrategia de la Democracia Cristiana en Centroamérica*, CINAS, Mexico City, September 1985, p.5.
7. Handy, *op.cit.*, p.171.
8. L. Frank and P. Wheaton, *Indian Guatemala: Path to Liberation*, EPICA, Washington 1984, p.51.
9. Mario Solórzano in *El Juego de los Reformismos*, Departamento Ecuménico de Investigaciones, Costa Rica, 1981, p.104.
10. Montenegro Ríos, *op.cit.*, p.31.
11. P. Berryman, *Christians in Guatemala's Struggle*, CIIR, London, 1984, p.70.
12. Handy, *op.cit.*, p.271.
13. Berryman, *op.cit.*, p.34.
14. M.A. Albizúrez, *El sindicalismo clasista entre dos fuegos*, Panorama, Mexico, 1986, p.19.
15. Frank and Wheaton, *op.cit.*, p.46.
16. J. Pearce, *Promised Land*, Latin America Bureau, London, 1986, p.99.

17. *El Gráfico*, Guatemala City, 8 June 1986.
18. Allan Nairn, in *The Nation*, 23 November 1985.
19. Latin American Regional Reports, *Mexico and Central America*, London, 14 August 1981.
20. *SIAG*, Mexico City, 18 January 1986, p.l.
21. Gaspar, *op.cit.*, p.15.
22. Inforpress, *Informe Especial*, Guatemala City, 3 July 1986.
23. *Ibid*, p.2.

Chapter 4: Cerezo's Choice

1. Inforpress, *Guatemala: Elections 1985*, Guatemala City, October 1985, p.11.
2. George Black, *Garrison Guatemala*, London, Zed 1984, p.190.
3. Inforpress, *op.cit.*, p.35.
4. NACLA, *Under the Gun*, November-December 1985, pp.21-2.
5. *Financial Times*, London, 12 December 1985.
6. WOLA and the International Human Rights Law Group, *The 1985 Elections: Will the Military Relinquish Power?*, Washington DC, December 1985, p.vii.
7. *Inforpress*, 28 November 1985.
8. Allan Nairn, *Village Voice*, 12 November 1985.
9. Víctor Perera, 'Can Guatemala Change?', *New York Review of Books*, 14 August 1986, p.39.
10. Francis Pisani, in *Le Monde Diplomatique*, Paris, June 1986, p.12.
11. Americas Watch and the British Parliamentary Human Rights Group (PHRG), *Human Rights in Guatemala During President Cerezo's First Year*, London and New York, February 1987, p.11.
12. Allan Nairn and Jean-Marie Simon, 'The Bureaucracy of Death', *New Republic*, 30 June 1986, p.16.
13. Americas Watch/PHRG, *op.cit.*, p.81.
14. *Ibid*, p.27.
15. Allan Nairn, in *New York Times*, 4 April 1983.
16. Nairn and Simon, *op.cit.*, p.14.
17. Jane Slaughter, *Labour Notes*, Detroit, October 1987.
18. Pisani, *op.cit.*, p.13.
19. Lord Avebury, *Guatemalan Elections: Fiction and Reality*, London, CIIR 1985, p.5.
20. Americas Watch/PHRG, *op.cit.*, p.45.
21. CERIGUA, Mexico City, *Vistazo Mensual*, October 1986, p.7.
22. *La Palabra*, Guatemala City, 31 December 1985.
23. Americas Watch/PHRG, *op.cit.*, pp.37 ff.
24. *Ibid*, p.60.
25. Jane Slaughter, *op.cit.*.
26. Inforpress, *Informe Especial*, Guatemala City, 19 June 1986.
27. *This Week*, 19 January 1987.

28. R. Wilson-Grau, *Guatemala Hoy*, (mimeo), Guatemala City, 1986, p.9.
29. *Inforpress*, 19 February 1987.
30. *Caribbean Insight*, London, May 1986, p.13.
31. *Caribbean Insight*, February 1986, p.15.
32. *Inforpress*, 6 November 1986.
33. *Inforpress*, 15 January 1987.
34. *Caribbean Insight*, October 1986, p.15.
35. *Inforpress*, 29 January 1987.
36. *Inforpress*, 31 July, 1986.
37. *Inforpress*, 30 October 1986.
38. *Inforpress*, 16 October 1986.
39. CITGUA, *Un Año Después*, Mexico City, January 1987, p.106.
40. *Enfoprensa*, Mexico City, 23 – 29 January 1987.
41. *This Week*, 2 February 1987.
42. *Caribbean Insight*, September 1986, p.13.
43. *Caribbean Insight*, *ibid*, p.14.
44. *Inforpress*, 20 November 1986.
45. Inforpress, *Informe Especial*, Guatemala City, 16 October 1986.
46. Americas Watch/PHRG, *op.cit.*, p.70.
47. Allan Nairn, in *The Progressive*, May 1986, pp.20 ff.
48. *Caribbean Insight*, December 1986, p.16.
49. *Inforpress*, 27 November 1986.
50. *This Week*, 16 February 1987.

Conclusion: Peace — An Impossible Dream?

1. *Le Monde Diplomatique*, Mexico City, January 1987, p.4.
2. *Inforpress*, 19 February 1987.

INDEX

LAB BOOKS ON CENTRAL AMERICA

Soft Drink, Hard Labour: Guatemalan Workers Take on Coca-Cola
Miguel Angel Reyes and Mike Gatehouse

Covers the recent history of the struggle of the Coca-Cola workers in Guatemala against their management, including the 1984 occupation, the general political and trade union context behind it, and Coca-Cola's local and international response to it. Most importantly, the booklet focuses on the way in which a small union can successfully take on a major multinational company by extremely careful local and international organisation.

40pp ISBN 0 906156 33 5 £0.95

Promised Land: Peasant Rebellion in Chalatenango, El Salvador
Jenny Pearce

'. . . traces the history of this northern Salvadorean province from the colonial period to today's insurgent war. Based on extensive research and a visit to guerrilla-held regions of Chalatenango in 1984, this book examines the economic pressures that pushed the peasantry to desperation, and the political evolution behind the revolutionary war. Pearce's book supplies a degree of depth and specificity about the situation in the Salvadorean *campo* not previously available in English. It discusses the dynamics of the war, and also provides an excellent agrarian reform case study, covering unsuccessful reformist efforts from the sixties to the eighties . . .' *Washington Report on the Hemisphere*

Includes oral histories from the people of Chalatenango and a prologue by the Salvadorean writer, Manlio Argueta.

320pp ISBN 0 906156 21 1 £6.95/US$12.95

Honduras: State for Sale
Richard Lapper and James Painter

Details the transformation of Honduras from banana enclave to the linchpin of US military strategy in the region. It identifies the elements which distinguish Honduras from its neighbours and explores the reasons why endemic poverty has not yet generated violent social conflict. The book examines the way US influence has affected political and economic developments since 1980, making a solution to the country's abject poverty more remote than ever.

132pp ISBN 0 906156 23 8 £3.50/US$7.00

Under the Eagle: US Intervention in Central America and the Caribbean

Jenny Pearce

From President Monroe to Reagan, **Under the Eagle** examines the history and motivations of US policy in Central America and the Caribbean and assesses its impact on the impoverished people of the region.
  Now in its fourth printing, 20,000 copies sold worldwide.

295pp ISBN 0 906156 13 0   **£5.95/US$10.00**

Book orders (plus 20% for post and packing please) to: **LAB, 1 Amwell Street, London EC1R 1UL**. Complete booklist available on request.

Under The Eagle is published in the USA by South End Press, Boston. All other LAB books are distributed in North America by Monthly Review Foundation, 155 West 23 Street, New York NY10011.

The Latin America Bureau is a small, independent non-profit making research organisation established in 1977. LAB is concerned with human rights and related social, political and economic issues in Central and South America and the Caribbean. We carry out research and publish books, publicise and lobby on these issues and establish support links with Latin American groups. We also brief the media, organise seminars and have a growing programme of schools publications.

Latin America Bureau
1 Amwell Street
London EC1R 1UL
Tel: 01-278 2829

CIIR For justice and development

CIIR PUBLISHES books and pamphlets on international social, economic and political issues, including the well-known *Comment* series.

CIIR SPEAKS OUT against injustice and oppression; its education work is rooted in the social teaching of the Catholic Church.

CIIR RECRUITS professional and technically qualified people to share their skills with local workers in Third World development projects.

CIIR NEEDS YOUR SUPPORT! Send £10.00 for one year's membership (£5.00 unwaged, £15.00 overseas) to CIIR, 22 Coleman Fields, London N1 7AF.

Institute of Latin American Studies

31 Tavistock Square

London WC1H 9HA.